the Prosocial GANG

Dedicated with admiration and appreciation to our trainers: Eloise Perez, Mary Sylva, Lynette Orr, James Martucci, Andria Jackson, Joseph Grossman; and our trainees: The Lo Lives, The Sammy Dreds, The Baby Wolfpack, The Brothers' Keepers, The Avenue U Boys, The Kings Highway Boys, The Neck Road Boys, The Bay Road, The Deceptanets, The Brownsville Girls.

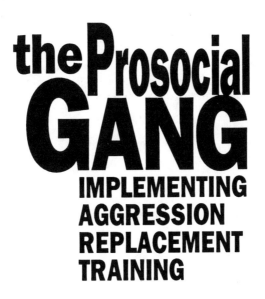

the Prosocial GANG

IMPLEMENTING AGGRESSION REPLACEMENT TRAINING

Arnold P. Goldstein
Barry Glick
with Wilma Carthan & Douglas A. Blancero

SAGE Publications
International Educational and Professional Publisher
Thousand Oaks   London   New Delhi

For information address:

SAGE Publications, Inc.
2455 Teller Road
Thousand Oaks, California 91320

SAGE Publications Ltd.
6 Bonhill Street
London EC2A 4PU
United Kingdom

SAGE Publications India Pvt. Ltd.
M-32 Market
Greater Kailash I
New Delhi 110 048 India

Printed in the United States of America

Library of Congress Cataloging-in-Publication Data

Goldstein, Arnold P.
    The prosocial gang: Implementing aggression replacement therapy /
authors Arnold P. Goldstein, Barry Glick with Wilma Carthan, Douglas A.
Blancero.
        p. cm.
    Includes bibliographical references and index.
    ISBN 0-8039-5770-X (cloth). — ISBN 0-8039-5771-8 (pbk.)
    1. Gangs—United States.   2. Juvenile delinquency—United States.
3. Juvenile delinquency—United States—Prevention   I. Glick, Barry.   II. Title.
HV6439.U5G654   1994
364.1'06'0973—dc20   94-8569

94 95 96 97 98   10 9 8 7 6 5 4 3 2 1

Sage Production Editor: Diana E. Axelsen

The research reported in this book was supported by Research Grant DCJS #JJ91411000 from the New York State Division of Criminal Justice Services. Their assistance and encouragement are very much appreciated.

Contents

Preface

Rock Brigade
Harlem Ranger Cadet Corps
Black Crusaders
Brothers Gaining Equality through Excellence
Nighthawks
Federación de Barrios Unidos
Puerto Rican Young Lords
East Harlem Youth Action Program
Brown Berets
Homeboy Tortillas

The phrase *prosocial gang*—both the title and organizing theme of this book—appears on its face to be an obvious contradiction. Gangs, we all know, are antisocial, not prosocial. The world of criminal justice asserts this, the media proclaim it daily, and, as later chapters will demonstrate, a great deal of sociological, psychological, and other data clearly affirm and describe such anti-socialness. Juvenile gangs, the consensus has it, are bad; they regularly commit an array of aggressive and criminal acts, and ought to be discouraged, disbanded, and dispersed. America, responding to this anti-gang consensus, is increasingly mobilized to reduce gang membership and gang activities. Unlike the 1950s and 1960s, when social workers were the country's primary gang-relevant professionals, and detached (from the agency or office) street work was the primary intervention activity, the police are today's gang specialists, and intelligence-gathering, deterrence, arrest, and incarceration are their gang-relevant pursuits. The change grew from several sources, but most especially from the heightened and often lethal gang-initiated violence that has so frequently characterized America's drug marketplaces and streets.

Also contributing to this shift, however, was the purported failure of detached worker programming. As we will illustrate in detail in Chapter 3, the central goal of such street work intervention was value transformation. Working with the gang as a unit whenever possible or with substantial cliques thereof, detached workers employed an array of counseling, vocational, and recreational techniques and activities in order to enhance gang youths' problem-solving skills, autonomy, self-esteem, cooperativeness, and competence vis-à-vis "conventional" behaviors. Stated most generally, value transformation was the hoped-for route to the prosocial gang.

It was a notion with great inherent appeal, and by the early 1960s, many dozens of American cities had ongoing, detached worker programs. Several evaluations of their effectiveness then followed and, to the surprise of many workers—given the then popularity of the approach—most such evaluations were negative. Results seemed to be consistently indicating that gang youth values and delinquent behavior were *not* favorably impacted by detached worker programming. Worse, some claimed that by working with the gang as a unit, workers were providing it with added recognition and legitimacy and thereby increasing its cohesiveness and durability. As a result of such findings and interpretations, detached worker youth gang interventions rapidly faded away, to be replaced by more individualized approaches designed for, among other purposes, weaning youth away from gang membership.

We describe these gang intervention activities and evaluations in detail later in this book, but wish to anticipate this later discussion by asserting here our belief that detached worker programming was not a failure and that, in fact, its efficacy remains unknown. As Klein (1968b) courageously describes vis-à-vis his own detached worker program, and as we strongly suspect was true for the large majority of such efforts, the actual worker-youth programming very frequently never took place. Klein's "detached" workers, for example, spent 25% to 50% of their time attached, in the agency, not the streets; 25% of their time travelling to and from their assigned neighborhood or waiting around, alone on the street; and only approximately 25% of the time engaged in actual activities with gang youths. Given caseload size, this translated to approximately 5 minutes per youth per week. Far from proving the ineffectiveness of detached worker programming, and its value transformation rationale, such failure of program implementation more parsimoniously suggests an indeterminacy of effectiveness. Even if carefully planned and evaluated, as many such programs were, if only carried forth minimally, its effectiveness is yet to be determined.

Add to this (non)finding and (non)refutation of the value transformation strategy two apparent facts: First, current criminal justice, "weed and seed" efforts to arrest gang leadership, in the hope that the gang as a then leaderless organization will dissolve, have rarely succeeded. Instead, youths rapidly coalesce around new leadership, or old leadership continues undeterred by incarceration. Second, boys need other boys. The need for a like-minded, compatible peer group exists, and further is a healthy, normal quality of adolescence in particular. These several factors, namely, the general failure of criminal justice "gang-busting" efforts, the legitimacy and even desirability of adolescent peer groups, and the apparent indeterminacy of effectiveness for earlier, gang youth value transformation efforts combine to serve as the strategic underpinning for the project we describe in this book. It is, as will be seen, an effort to work with a series of intact gangs, as gangs, in order to move their members in more constructive directions and begin creating a series of prosocial gangs.

Thus, for us, the phrase *prosocial gang* clearly is not a contradiction. This chapter opens with a list of such youth groups, and others exist. Some were prosocial in intent and action from their beginning. Others formed first into a juvenile gang, engaged for an often extended period of time in illegal behaviors, and then, through various combinations of their own and agency/community worker efforts, shifted in both their overt behaviors and underlying attitudes toward distinctly prosocial standards. Such movement has happened in the past, and can be facilitated in the future. This book is a journey into one such facilitative attempt.

We open with a series of chapters that seek to provide a comprehensive context for our own program. The history of juvenile gangs in America is our initial focus. Their development, demographics, varying definitions, and types will each be considered. Our society's long-standing negative view of juvenile gangs is primarily a function of the persistence and growth of gang violence. As the rumble of yesteryear has been replaced by the lethal drive-by shooting of today, community awareness and response have very markedly intensified. Chapter 2 examines this central feature of gang life and behavior. The levels and forms of gang violence are considered, as is its diverse extrinsic and intrinsic sources. Perhaps most noteworthy in this consideration is the shift in recent years from gang violence as territorial (neighborhood) defense, to its employment for the establishment and protection of (drug) market share.

For 50 years America has been seeking to respond effectively and constructively to such gang violence. Four phases of gang intervention programming are discernible, and are the focus of Chapter 3—detached street work, opportunity provision and social infusion, opportunity withdrawal and social control, and what we have termed comprehensive programming. The substance, strengths, and apparent weaknesses of each phase will be described, as well as how social/political climate combined with gang behavior in America in each instance to cause the demise of one intervention phase and the apparent necessity for the next.

Consideration of our contribution to this intervention stream, Aggression Replacement Training (ART), is then presented. Chapter 4 describes its background, its rationale, and its specific constituent procedures. ART was first developed and implemented by us in 1984, and following its introduction both we and others have had several opportunities to evaluate its effectiveness with delinquent and aggressive youths. These past efficacy evaluations will be presented and examined in Chapter 5. Chapter 6 introduces the present program, the use and evaluation of ART with a series of intact juvenile gangs. The 10 gangs are compositely described in this chapter, as is a sense of the daily lives of their members, their communities, and the agency settings in which the program unfolded. Chapter 7 depicts the program itself, its administration and implementation. Here we offer the reader a full sense of its construction, its management, its contents, its flow, its successes, and its failures. We seek here to offer means for prosocially motivating chronically antisocial youths, for dealing with attendance indifference, participation resistance, interpersonal skill incompetence, anger impatience, and much more. Chapter 7 is, in short, a "nuts and bolts" statement of our program's direction and management.

Building upon both the earlier, formal evaluations of ART presented in Chapter 6, and its qualitative documentation based on observation, and staff session notes, we also present in the chapter a comprehensive, quantitative, and qualitative evaluation of program efficacy. Does ART change gang youth behavior-interpersonal skills, anger responsiveness, prosocial and antisocial behavior in real-life settings, incidence of arrest? These are the questions our formal data analyses address.

In the book's final chapter, we both summarize and look ahead, seeking to draw out both the policy and the programmatic implications of our findings at this point in the history of juvenile ganging in America. It is our hope and aspiration throughout these chapters to not only share our ART journey into the domain of the gang, but to also more broadly offer a partial roadway for traversing difficult and challenging program implementation and evaluation territory.

I

Introduction

1

Gangs in the United States

The gang has been viewed as a play group as well as a criminal organization (Puffer, 1912; Thrasher, 1963); also as malicious and negativistic, comprising mainly younger adolescents (Cohen, 1955); or representing different types of delinquent subcultural adaptation (Cloward & Ohlin, 1960). Definitions in the 1950s and 1960s were related to issues of etiology as well as based on liberal, social reform assumptions. Definitions in the 1970s and 1980s are more descriptive, emphasizing violent and criminal characteristics, and possibly reflecting a more conservative philosophy of social control and deterrence (Klein & Maxson, 1989). The most recent trend may be to view gangs as more pathological than functional and to restrict usage of the term to a narrow set of violent and criminal groups (Spergel, Ross, Curry, & Chance, 1989, p. 13).

Spergel et al.'s (1989) brief overview captures well the development and diversity of gang definitions. Many definitions have been put forward during the past 80 years, and in a real sense *all* are correct. What constitutes a gang has varied with time and place, with political and economic conditions, with community tolerance and community conservatism, with the level and nature of police and citizen concern, with cultural and subcultural traditions and mores, and with media-generated sensationalism or indifference to law-violating youth groups.

Miller (1974) conducted a survey of 160 criminal justice and youth service agencies, inquiring into their respective definitions of "gang." Six major elements were more or less agreed on:

1. Being organized
2. Having identifiable leadership
3. Identifying with a territory

4   THE PROSOCIAL GANG

4. Associating continuously
5. Having a specific purpose
6. Engaging in illegal activities

Thus, in part, "What is a gang?" may be answered by reference to these half-dozen qualities. Interestingly, substantial regional differences in gang organization, and hence definition, have become apparent. In California, and in those regions most heavily influenced by California gangs, gangs are, as Miller (1974) concluded, largely characterized by structured organization, identifiable leadership, territorial identification, continuous association, specific purpose, and engagement in illegal behavior. In New York City, the venue for the present project, gangs tend to be loosely organized, of changeable leadership, criminally active, and not territorially oriented; they associate irregularly, pursue amorphous purposes, and engage in not only illegal, but also legal activities. In all regions, however, they are often more violent and more drug-involved, and these two characteristics must also be included prominently in establishing an accurate, contemporary definition of *gang* in America.

In addition to seeking directly to define *gang* as both a term and a phenomenon, its meaning may be clarified further by noting, as shown in Table 1.1, a series of relevant definitional distinctions, drawn from the work of Spergel and Curry (1990).

How else may the nature of delinquent youth gangs in the United States best be clarified? In the sections that follow we will seek to do so by examining their history, current gang demographics, bases for their membership motivation, and typical gang behaviors.

History

Delinquent ganging in 20th-century America did not emerge de novo, but grew from a long and varied American tradition of group violence. Between 1760 and 1900, 500 vigilante groups—the Ku Klux Klan, the White Cappers, the Black Legion prominent among them—appeared in the United States (Gurr, 1989). Whippings, bombings, arson, and murder were among their violent tools for terrorizing ethnic and religious minorities and other targets of their hate. Less organized, but directed toward similar violent ends, were lynch mobs, responsible for taking the lives of 3,400 black Americans between 1882 and 1951 (Gurr, 1989). Piracy; banditry; feuding; labor, agrarian, and

TABLE 1.1 Definitional Distinctions

---

1. Gang
2. Street gang   (Youth and adult; emphasis on location)
3. Posse/Crew   (Loosely organized group in the process of forming a gang; often involved in drug trafficking)
4. Copy-cat gang   (Media-inspired; ephemeral; minor delinquencies)
5. Pretend gang   (Elementary age youths; a "play" activity)
6. Gang clique   (A "tight" gang subgroup; a gang age-cohort)
7. Delinquent youth groups   (Less organized than gang; less serious violations; very common)
8. Criminal organization   (Youth and adult)
9. Street group   (Street clubs; youth organizations; social and athletic clubs)

SOURCE: Spergel & Curry (1990)

race riots; and the frequently glamorized marauding bands of frontier out-laws, such as Butch Cassidy's High Five and the Jesse James gang, are each in their own ways ancestors of the contemporary American gang (Brown, 1980). The Forty Thieves, an Irish-American immigrant gang formed in 1820 in the Five Points District of New York City, is cited by the Illinois State Police (1989) as the first modern (adult) criminal gang. It gave rise, as did many of the adult gangs that followed, to an "auxiliary" or "sub-gang" of juveniles, in this first instance called the Forty Little Thieves. Other such adult and juvenile gangs quickly followed, the Kerryonians, the Dusters, the Plug Uglies, the Dead Rabbits, and so on (Asbury, 1971).

As the American population spread westward, so too did the delinquent gang. Some of these early gangs, reflecting the definitions of the day, were largely mischievous play groups, for example Sheldon's (1898, cited in Furfey, 1926) secret clubs, social clubs, and predatory organizations; Puffer's (1912) clubs and athletic teams; and Furfey's (1926) adolescent groups. But with the passage of time and the growing influence of adult criminal behavior, as well as a number of other societal forces, "gang" took on increasingly darker tones. Thrasher's (1927) landmark study of 1,313 Chicago-area gangs, antici-pating later emergence of labeling theory, sought to depict how such "play groups" evolved into delinquent gangs:

> It does not become a gang, however, until it begins to excite disapproval and opposition. It discovers a rival or an enemy in the gang in the next block; its baseball or football team is pitted against some other team; parents or neigh-bors look upon it with suspicion or hostility; . . . the storekeeper or the cops begin to give it shags [chase it]; or some representative of the community steps in and tries to break it up. This is the real beginning of the gang, for now it starts to draw itself more closely together. It becomes a conflict group. (p. 26)

Thrasher's (1963) study was truly seminal, in many instances offering for the first time insights and dimensions of concern that remain yet today the topics of relevance in contemporary discussions of gangs and gang behavior. The complexity of the roots of gang formation, ganging as a process, situational gang leadership, the influence on gang organization and behavior of community forces, and the role of what later came to be called groupthink in gang functioning were each anticipated in the writings of Thrasher. Other early members of the "Chicago School of Sociology" built significantly on Thrasher's work. Bolitho (1930), Landesco (1932), and Tannenbaum (1938), for example, each provided further description of the organization and functioning of Chicago's delinquent gangs, and further elaboration of several of Thrasher's central conclusions.

Thinking about causation, that is, *why* gangs form, changed over the course of this period of early gang research. In its beginning, reflecting the heavy reliance on both Darwinian theorizing and instinct as the core explanatory construct in the behavioral science of the day, Puffer (1912) asserted:

> We must, then, so far as we are good evolutionists, look upon the boy's gang as the result of a group of instincts inherited from a distant past. . . . we must suppose that these gang instincts arose in the first because they were useful once, and that they have been preserved to the present day because they are, on the whole, useful still. (p. 83)

Thrasher (1963) looked for causative explanation within both the youths themselves and the community of which the youths were a part. The typical gang member, in his view, was "a rather healthy, well-adjusted, red-blooded American boy seeking an outlet for normal adolescent drives for adventure and expression" (Hardman, 1967, p. 7). Yet, the youths' environment was equally important to Thrasher. Inadequacies in family functioning, schools, housing, sanitation, employment and other community characteristics combined to help motivate youths to turn elsewhere—to the gang—for life satisfactions and rewards. This focus on social causation blossomed fully during the next era of gang research, the 1930s into the early 1940s, which Hardman (1967) appropriately labeled "the Depression studies." It was an era in which social scientists sought explanation for many of America's ills—including delinquent ganging—in "social causation, social failure, social breakdown" (Hardman, 1967, p. 9). Landesco (1932) emphasized the effects of conflicting immigrant and American cultures. Shaw and McKay (1942) more complexly stressed a combination of slum area deterioration, poverty, family dissolution, and organized crime. Tannenbaum (1938) analogously proposed that the gang forms not because of its attractiveness per se, but because "positive sociocultural forces"—family, school, church—that might train a youth into more socially acceptable behaviors are weak or unavailable. Wattenberg and Balistrieri (1950) similarly stressed socioeconomically substandard neighborhoods and lax parental supervision. In the same contextual explanatory spirit, Bogardus (1943)—in one of the first West Coast gang studies—emphasized the war and warlike climate in America as underpinning the aggressive gangs forming at that time. Dumpson (1949), more multicausal but still contextual in his causative thinking, identified the war, racism, and diverse political and economic sources.

Edgerton (1988) summarizes this stream of social causation thinking well in his assertion that the essential factors contributing importantly to the formation of gangs include:

> Residential segregation in low-income areas, poverty, poor school performance, little parental supervision, discrimination, and distrust of law enforcement. In these conditions, young people spent much of their lives together on the streets where a gang served them . . . as surrogate family, school, and police. We also hear from gang members . . . about the appeal that gang membership has for them—friendship, pride, prestige, belongingness, identity, self-esteem, and a desire to emulate their uncles and older brothers who were gang members before them. (p. x)

Current Gang Demographics

Accurate data on the number, nature, structure, and functioning of delinquent gangs are hard to come by. No national-level agency has assumed responsibility for the systematic collection and reporting of gang-relevant information. Each city or region is free to and does formulate its own definition of "gang," and decides what gang-relevant data to collect. Police (who are the major source of gang information in most American cities), public service agencies, schools, mass media representatives, and others regularly exposed to gang youths not infrequently exaggerate or minimize their numbers and illegal behaviors as a function of political, financial, or other impression management needs. Compounding the difficulty in obtaining adequate, accurate, objective, and relevant information are gang youths themselves. Hagedorn and Macon (1988) comment:

Be wary of your information. Gang members are quite adept at telling social
workers and policemen self-serving lies. Glib misinformation is, in fact, a
survival tool for many gang members. It is easy for outside people (and that
is practically everybody) to believe social workers and policemen because
they have direct contact with gang members. Yet this direct contact is often
managed by the gang members themselves, sometimes for survival, sometimes even for self-glorifying exaggeration, and police and gang workers
also have some self-interest in the images they purvey. (p. 4)

Thus, caution in accepting the available data and conservatism in its interpretation are requisite. Given these provisos, what is currently known about
the structure and demographics of the contemporary delinquent gang?

As noted earlier, in 1974 Miller conducted a major, national survey seeking
gang-relevant information from a spectrum of public and private service
agencies, police departments, probation offices, courts, juvenile bureaus, and
similar sources. Particular attention was paid in this effort to the six American cities reporting the highest levels of gang activity. Philadelphia and Los
Angeles reported the highest proportion of gang members to their respective
male adolescent populations (6 per 100). For the other survey cities, comparable ratios were New York (4 per 100), Chicago (2 per 100), Detroit and San
Francisco (less than 1 per 100). The combined rate for all six cities was 37
per 1,000, or approximately 4%. Overall numerical estimates, for the group
of six cities, ranged from a low of 760 gangs with 28,500 members, to 2,700
gangs with 81,500 members. As has consistently been reported in earlier
decades, gang members in the surveyed cities were predominantly male; age
12 to 21; residing in the poorer, usually central city areas;[1] and came from
families at the lower occupational and educational levels. Gang youths
were African American ($\frac{1}{2}$), Hispanic ($\frac{1}{6}$), Asian ($\frac{1}{10}$), and non-Hispanic white
($\frac{1}{10}$), and strongly tended to form themselves into ethnically homogeneous
gangs.

Needle and Stapleton (1982) surveyed police departments in 60 American
cities of various sizes. Half the cities with populations between 250,000 and
500,000, and more than one-third of the cities with between 100,000 and
250,000 people reported gang problems. Delinquent youth gangs were no
longer to be seen as only a big-city problem. Though the popular mythology
of this spread is that most such non-big-city gangs are branches intentionally
exported to such locations by particular big-city gangs or mega-gangs (especially Los Angeles's Crips and Bloods), the reality appears a bit more complex.
While a modest amount of such "franchising," "branching," or "hiving off"
apparently occurs, most midsize and smaller city gangs appear to either

originate in such locations or are started by nonresident gang members via kinship, alliance, the expansion of turf boundaries, or the movement of gang members' families into new areas (Moore, Vigil, & Garcia, 1983).

By 1989, according to yet another, and particularly extensive, survey conducted by Spergel, Ross, Curry, and Chance (1989), delinquent gangs were located in almost all 50 states, a few in the north-central mountains and perhaps northeastern United States being possible exceptions. As a group, 35 surveyed cities reported 1,439 gangs. California, Illinois, and Florida especially had substantial gang concentrations. Spergel et al. report that three jurisdictions in particular have especially high numbers of youth gangs: Los Angeles County (600), Los Angeles City (280), and Chicago (128). Of the total of 120,636 gang members reported to exist in all the surveyed cities combined, 70,000 were estimated to be in Los Angeles County, including 26,000 in the city of Los Angeles; 12,000 were estimated to be in Chicago.[2] But it is clearly not only these three jurisdictions expressing concern. Spergel et al. report that while 14% of their survey's law enforcement respondents and 8% of other respondents believed that the gang situation in their respective jurisdictions had improved since 1980, 56% of the police and 68% of the non-law enforcement respondents claimed that their situation had worsened.

Males continue to outnumber female gang members at a ratio of approximately 20 to 1. Gang size is a variable function of a number of determinants, including density of the youth population in a given geographical or psychological area (i.e., the pool to draw on), the nature of the gang's activities, police pressures, season of the year, gang recruitment efforts, relevant agency activity, and additional factors (Spergel, 1965). Approximately 5% or less of gang crime is committed by females. Females join gangs later than do males, and leave earlier. The age range of gang membership appears to have expanded, to from 9 to 30 or older, as gang involvement in drug dealing has increased. Younger members are often used as lookouts, runners, and so on, with the knowledge that if they are caught, judges and juvenile law tend to be more lenient when the perpetrator is younger. Older members tend to remain in the gang as a result of both the profitability of drug dealing and the paucity of employment opportunities for disadvantaged populations in the legitimate economy. Blacks, Hispanics, Asians, and whites are America's gang members.[3] Spergel et al. (1989) report a degree of specialization in the nature of the criminal behavior predominantly engaged in by these ethnically different gangs: "Black gangs are more involved in drug trafficking, Hispanic groups in turf-related battling, Asians in a variety of property crimes, and Whites in both organized property crimes and vandalism" (p. 239). Such

semi-specialization, Spergel et al. assert, may result more from accultur-
ation patterns, access to criminal opportunities, and community stability than
ethnicity per se. White gangs appear to be particularly diverse in their
organizing foci—motorcycle gangs or bikers, stoners, heavy metal groups,
satanic worshipers, neo-Nazi groups, fighting gangs.

Huff (1989) conducted a comprehensive gang survey of police chiefs in
the state of Ohio. Cleveland (50 gangs) and Columbus (20 gangs) were that
state's leading gang centers. These gangs appear to have originated mostly
from either earlier formed break dancing/rap groups or street corner groups
that evolved into gangs via increasing conflictual competition with similar
groups.

Why do youths join gangs? Their multiple motivations seem to differ very
little from why all adolescents reach out to peer groups for important life
satisfactions. Gang membership is sought for camaraderie, pride, identity
development, enhancement of self-esteem, acquisition of resources, support,
excitement, and related typical adolescent goals. Such goals reflect normal,
healthy adolescent aspirations. Unfortunately, for many gang youths, the
fulfillment of such aspirations is often sought by antisocial means. Actual
recruitment into membership, Jankowski (1991) reports, is usually of one of
three types. Fraternity-like recruitment resembles a fraternity "rush," in
which existing members and inquiring nonmembers meet to "look each other
over" and, if both like what they see, membership usually follows. Obliga-
tory (to community) recruitment typically occurs in neighborhoods contain-
ing gangs that have been in existence for many generations. "Grandpa and
I, your father, were in the gang. So, too, your brother and cousins. So it is
expected that you too will join." Finally, coercive recruitment takes place
when existing members—perhaps in response to the presence of larger, rival
gangs in adjacent neighborhoods—forcefully inform a same neighborhood
nonmember that he must join or leave the neighborhood.

What do gangs do? Mostly they just "hang out," engaging as we will see
in the diverse interpersonal behaviors characteristic of almost all adolescents. They also commit delinquent acts and engage in various forms and
levels of aggressive behavior, activities we will examine in depth later in this
book. In order to claim and topographically define their turf or territory, they
may make (sometimes extensive) use of graffiti—often in the form of a wall
painting of the gang's name, members' names, and/or the gang's symbol.
Graffiti may also be used to challenge or show contempt for a rival gang, by

crossing out the latter's graffiti, or by drawing it oneself but backward or upside-down. As part of its central effort to create both we-ness (within the gang) and difference (from other gangs), gang members will often incorporate distinctive colors or color combinations within their dress; make use of special hand signs as a means of communicating (especially the gang's name); and engage in representing, that is, wearing one's clothes in such a manner that either the left or right side of one's body is emphasized. A recent report by the Illinois State Police (1989) captures well these (often highly elaborate) efforts at creating distinctiveness:

> The Discipline Nation and their affiliates . . . refer to themselves as the Folks, their major insignia is the Six Pointed Star, and their dress is "right." Their basic color is black and if they wear an earring it will be in the right ear. They wear their hat tilted to the right and one of their favorite hats is the blue Civil War cap, they will wear one glove on the right hand, they may have one pocket on the right side turned inside out and it will be dyed in the gang's color or colors, they will roll up the right pants leg, they may have two of the fingernails on the right hand colored with the gang's colors, the hood of their sweatshirt will be dyed with the gang's colors, their shoes will either be colored or the laces of the right shoe will be in the gang's color, their belt buckle will be loose on the right side, and they may wear a bandanna in the gang's colors anywhere on the right side of their body. (pp. 9-10)

What else do gangs do? On occasion they fight, act aggressively, behave violently. While the absolute amount of such behavior is small, its effect on the chain of media response, public perception of gang youth behavior, and police and public agency countermeasures is quite substantial. In the chapter that follows we will examine more fully the sources, scope, and impact of such gang behavior.

Besides violence, gang members frequently engage in an array of entrepreneurial activities. Capitalizing on such entrepreneurial qualities as competitiveness, desire to accumulate money and possessions, status seeking, planning ability, and risk taking (Jankowski, 1991), gang youth engage in:

1. Selling drugs, liquor, auto parts, guns, electronic equipment
2. Protection, physical coercion
3. Demolition (arson)
4. Numbers, gambling rooms, cockfights
5. Muggings, purse snatchings, holdups, burglaries
6. Legal activities, for example, grocery stores, apartment rental, auto repair, hair shops

TABLE 1.2   Codes Regulating Member Behavior

1. Conflict behavior, e.g., hand-to-hand only
2. Personal relations with relatives and lovers
3. Clubhouse behavior
4. Consumption of drugs
5. Leadership abuse of power
6. Leadership change process
7. Offense-punishment specifications
8. Appropriate dress

SOURCE: Jankowski (1991)

Their hanging out, their aggression, their entrepreneurial efforts are all frequently guided by adherence to formal and informal codes designed to regulate member behavior, especially vis-à-vis other members of the same gang. Jankowski (1991) provides the common code targets (Table 1.2).

What are the primary membership paths? Though many "juvenile" gang members remain in their gang, as noted earlier, into their 30s and even 40s, most still marry-out, age-out, or job-out into the legitimate economy. Those core members most heavily committed during their adolescent years to membership and its illegal pursuits frequently shift to individual or organized crime careers. A great many go to prison. And a great many die violently.

Notes

1. In some of the surveyed cities, the slums from which the gang youths came had moved from their traditional center city location to ring-city or suburban areas. Still poor ghettos, but in new locations, these disproportionate sources of gang youths were often large-scale housing projects.

2. This numerical litany of youth participation in gangs should be tempered with the reminder that most youths, even in areas in which gangs are common, do not join gangs. Vigil (1983), for example, estimates that only 4% to 10% of Chicano youths are affiliated with gangs.

3. Membership strongly tends to continue, and often further solidify, when and if the gang youth is incarcerated (Camp & Camp, 1985; Jacobs, 1974; Lane, 1989). Gott (1989), for example, reports that in 1989 approximately 5,000 of the 9,000 youths incarcerated in California Youth Authority facilities were gang members and that, as others have observed, gang cohesiveness and activity level appear to be substantially accelerated by and during incarceration.

2

Gang Aggression

Juvenile gangs in early 20th-century America committed acts of theft, burglary and vandalism, but only rarely was there serious within—or between—gang fighting (Puffer, 1912; Thrasher, 1963). By the 1950s, fights between rival gangs had become somewhat more common. As Gardner (1983) observes:

> The gangs of the 1950s engaged in big fights called rumbles, which had definite arrangements and rules to be followed. Times, places, and uses of weapons were agreed upon in advance by the war council or leadership of the two warring gangs. Usually, the location chosen would be a deserted area of the city, where the police were not likely to discover them. In those days, gangs fought each other with bats, bricks, clubs, and chains. Occasionally, someone flashed a switchblade or used a homemade zip gun. (p. 23)

Their purposes were diverse: "to inflict humiliation and insult on the opposing group . . . to increase the victor's reputation and status . . . to regain territory [and] sometimes to gain new territories . . . to re-establish discipline . . . [in response to] boredom and apathy" (New York City Youth Board, 1960, p. 83).

Such fighting between entire gangs or gang members did occur, though their frequency and resultant damage were often exaggerated by the mass media, and sometimes by the participating youths themselves. Not infrequently, gang members anticipated such experiences with considerable ambivalence, but under considerable peer pressure as well as an overriding need to maintain "rep," proceeded to fight nevertheless. Sometimes, under rep-maintaining circumstances, the rumble was avoided. Spergel (1965) notes:

> Youngsters may literally pray silently that something will occur to prevent them from reaching their destination. Consequently, almost any excuse to

avoid contact with the opposing group may be utilized. The appearance of
the worker, the arrival of the police, or a sudden flat tire on a car which was
to take the group into enemy territory may be sufficient to prevent the spontaneous or planned attack. (p. 115)

Klein and Maxson (1989) similarly note: "In the 1950s and 1960s, gang
members talked much about their fighting episodes, but [homicide] data from
several projects revealed their bark to be worse than their bite" (p. 218).

Inter-gang member fighting took a variety of forms. The New York City
Youth Board's (1960) classification was:

> Fighting without weapons between two members of opposing groups.
> Fighting with weapons between two members of opposing groups.
> Fighting between a small group from one gang and a single member from another
>   gang.
> Fighting between two small groups.
> Fighting between two large groups.

Miller, in his 1975 national survey report, *Violence by Youth Gangs and
Youth Groups as a Crime Problem in Major American Cities,* offered the
following subtyping of assaultive gang member behaviors:

> Planned rumble, a prearranged encounter between sizable rival groups.
> Rumble, an encounter between sizable rival groups.
> Warfare, a continuing series of retaliatory engagements between members of rival
>   groups.
> Foray, in which smaller bands of youths engage rival bands.
> Hit, in which smaller bands of youths engage one or two rivals.
> Fair fight, in which a single gang member engages a single rival.

Sometimes, fighting between two gangs extended over long time periods and
several separate altercations. Horowitz (1983) comments:

> In seeking to protect and promote their reputations, gangs often engage in
> prolonged "wars," which are kept alive between larger fights by many small
> incidents and threats of violence. Following each incident one gang claims
> precedence, which means that the other group must challenge them if they
> want to retain their honor and reassert their reputation. (p. 94)

Gradually into and through the 1970s and 1980s, the levels and forms of
gang violence in the United States changed for the worse in parallel with the
levels and forms of violence elsewhere on the American scene. Whereas the

Roxbury Project (Miller, 1974), Group Guidance Project (Klein, 1971), and Ladino Hills Project (Klein, 1971) gang intervention programs of the 1950s and 1960s collectively revealed almost no homicides and only modest amounts of other types of gang violence, there were 81 gang-related homicides in Chicago in 1981, 351 such deaths in Los Angeles in 1980, and more than 1,500 in Los Angeles during the 1985-1989 period (Gott, 1989). Spergel et al. (1989) report that only about 1% of all the violent crime committed in Chicago was perpetrated by gang members. The seriousness of such figures, however, resides not only in their relative increase from past years, but especially in their nature—primarily homicide and aggravated assault. Such violent offenses, Spergel et al. observe, are three times more likely to be committed by gang members than by non-gang delinquents, a finding also reported by Friedman, Mann, and Friedman (1975) and Tracy (1979). In addition to the substantial levels of violent behavior directed by gang members toward persons or groups (gangs) outside their own gang, considerable amounts of aggression occur on an intra-gang basis. Miller, Geertz, and Cutter (1968) examined this phenomenon and set its occurrence at 70% of all gang member aggression. Of the 1,395 aggressive acts recorded during their observational period, 7% were physical attacks, and 65% were derogations, devaluations, or other directly hostile statements.

In our next section we will examine both fact and speculation regarding the reasons underlying this contemporary increase in violence between and within gangs. As far as the sheer amount of such behavior is concerned, however, the weight of evidence combines to suggest that delinquent gangs in America have indeed been behaving in a more violent manner in recent years. Nevertheless, it is important to note that such an apparent increase may derive, at least in part, from artifactual sources. Media interest in youth gangs ebbs and flows, and tends to be accentuated in direct proportion to youth violence levels. The contemporary increase in such behaviors may be partially just such a media interest effect. The likelihood of this possibility is enhanced by a second potential artifact, the relative absence of reliable sources of gang-relevant information. As Klein and Maxson (1989) note: "The 1960s gang programs, which permitted detailed description of gang structure and activity patterns, are now largely absent. . . . The current picture is based on evidence that is largely hearsay rather than empirical" (p. 209). Finally, following from the fact that by far the majority of the current gang-relevant information available comes from police sources, it is possible that information regarding increased gang violence is in part also an artifact of more, and more intensive, police department gang intelligence unit activity. Given these several evidential ambiguities, it seems most parsimonious to concur with Klein and Maxson (1989) who assert that "it remains unclear whether the observed violence increase reflects greater levels of violence among and between gangs, whether it is a result of a growth in the number of gangs or gang members, or whether it reflects an increasingly violent society" (p. 218).

Bases for Increased Violence

Elsewhere we have presented an extended rationale for the value of conceptualizing aggression complexly, as a multicausal, complexly determined, primarily learned set of behaviors (Goldstein, 1988). Conceptualizing aggression in this manner, we believe, both more accurately captures its diverse origins, and provides substantially enhanced opportunity (since its source is not located in its entirety in the perpetrator) for its remediation. In the present section, which seeks to identify bases for the increased levels of contemporary gang violence, we will seek to take a similarly complex, multicausal position. Thus, the bases enumerated and discussed below are to be seen as an additive combination of likely sources, and less as alternative explanations. It will also be apparent that the sources offered here are, as a group, consistent with the interactionist philosophy growing in popularity in contemporary psychology, a philosophy which holds that human behavior springs conjointly from characteristics of the individual actor and qualities of his or her environment.

Environmental Enhancers

Drugs. The major environmental enhancers of contemporary gang violence—in addition to the heightened general levels of aggression in American society today—appear to be drugs, territory, and guns. To an increasing degree, fighting is over drug selling and economic territory and less about neighborhood turf ownership and physical territory, though the latter still fuel their share of violent incidents. Competition for drug markets, at least in some regions of the United States, appears in fact to be an especially important source of gangs as aggressors. Huff (1993) describes the situation well:

> One strategy to discourage competitors for drug turf is to intimidate them into submission with brutal beatings, heinous murders, mutilations, and

other incidents of dramatic violence designed to shock competitors and ene-
mies. This strategy has especially been associated with Jamaican posses, but
it is used by youth gangs, drug gangs, and organized crime groups in connection with drug trafficking and the acquisition and protection of drug markets.
(pp. 9-10)

Territory. The traditional major source of gang violence—territoriality—
continues to be a relevant concern. Though enhanced mobility away from
one's turf via use of automobiles, dispersal of many school-age youths to schools
out of their home areas as a result of desegregation efforts, and enhanced
focus on economic rather than physical territory have all taken place, many
gangs continue to mark, define, claim, protect, and fight over their turf. Vigil
(1988) quotes one gang youth who powerfully makes this point:

> The only thing we can do is build our own little nation. We know that we have
> complete control in our community. It's like we're making our stand. . . . We're
> all brothers and nobody fucks with us. . . . We take pride in our little nation
> and if any intruders enter, we get panicked because we feel our community
> is being threatened. The only way is with violence. (p. 131)

With whom do they fight? Ley (1976) observes:

> Propinquity emerges as a critical factor in motivations for gang conflict. Of
> 188 gang incidents between 32 gangs in Philadelphia . . . (homicides, stab-
> bings, shootings and gang fights), 60 percent occurred between gangs who
> shared a common boundary and another 23 percent between gangs whose ter-
> ritories were two blocks or less apart. Only two incidents occurred between
> groups whose turfs were separated by more than 10 blocks. (pp. 262-263)

Miller (1982) suggests that such territorial defense seeks to protect both
identification and control, and can be manifested in three types of rights claimed
by the defending (or attacking) gang members:

1. Ownership rights, in which gang members claim, and are willing to fight for,
   ownership of the entire property and all activity within it, including who may
   enter, and who may leave.
2. Occupancy rights, in which gangs engage in shared use of a given territory
   under specified conditions, for example, when, for how long, for what purpose.
3. Enterprise monopoly rights, in which gangs claim exclusive rights to conduct
   certain criminal activities (theft, drug selling, and so on) within a specified
   territory.

Guns. There are 200 million privately owned guns in the United States (Goldstein, 1983). Since 1900 more than 750,000 American civilians have been killed by privately owned guns. Each year there are 200,000 gun-related injuries and approximately 20,000 gun-related deaths: 3,000 by accident, 7,000 by homicide, 9,000 by suicide. Guns are involved in two out of every three murders in America, one third of all robberies, and one fifth of all aggravated assaults. Such a remarkable level and use of weaponry has major implications for both the level and lethality of American gang violence. As noted earlier the gang rumbles of decades ago, whatever their group or individual expressions, typically involved utilization of fists, sticks, bricks, bats, pipes, knives, and an occasional homemade zip gun. The geometric proliferation of often sophisticated (automatic and semiautomatic) guns in America, and their ready availability have changed matters considerably (Fisher, 1976; Zimring, 1977). Klein and Maxson (1989) put it well:

> Does the ready access to guns explain much of the increase in violence? The notion here is that more weapons yield more shootings; these, in turn, lead to more "hits"; and these, in turn, lead to more retaliations in a series of reciprocal actions defending honor and territory. . . . The theory is that firearms have been the teeth that transform bark into bite. (p. 219)

In a commentary aptly titled *When the Trigger Pulls the Finger,* Berkowitz (n.d.) summarizes a series of investigations (Berkowitz & LePage, 1967; Leyens & Parke, 1975; Turner, Simons, Berkowitz, & Frodi, 1977) pointing to a second means (beyond sheer number) by which guns may provoke, not only express, overt aggression. These studies appear to demonstrate that:

> weapons stimulate people to act aggressively because of their aggressive meaning. In other words, many of us associate guns with the idea of killing and hurting. Because of these associations, the mere sight of a weapon can elicit thoughts, feelings and perhaps even muscular reactions in us that we have previously learned to connect with aggressive behavior. If we do not have any strong inhibitions against aggression at that moment, these elicited thoughts, feelings and motor reactions can heighten the chances that we will show open aggression toward others who happen to be available. (Berkowitz, n.d., pp. 2-3)

Gang Member Qualities

There appear to be a number of characteristics of contemporary American gang members, which, when combined with the environmental enhancers just described, contribute importantly to the observed increases in current gang violence.

Number and age. Two such characteristics are straightforwardly demographic: more gangs and older gang members. Both Klein and Maxson (1989) and Spergel et al. (1989) have speculated that these qualities may themselves help account for the apparently heightened levels of gang violence. There may also be a relevant interaction between weapons by gang member age:

> The older age of gang members may also be responsible for greater use of sophisticated weaponry and consequent violence. More and better weaponry may be [more] available to older teenagers and young adults than to juveniles. The median age of the gang homicide offender has been 19 years . . . in Chicago for the past ten years (Spergel, 1986). Los Angeles data (Maxson, Gordon, & Klein, 1985) and San Diego police statistics (San Diego Association of Governments, 1982) also indicate that older adolescents and young adults are mainly involved in gang homicide. Younger gang members are engaged in a pattern of gang assault which leads to less lethal consequences. (Spergel et al., 1989)[1]

Honor. Honor and its several related, long-established gang youth characteristics, such as machismo, self-esteem, status, power, heart, and reputation, are purported to contribute importantly to overt aggression. Perhaps they do so even more today. Miller (1982) wonders if honor has become less of a factor in the etiology of gang member aggression. As such aggression has changed in form and frequency from inter-gang rumbles defending local turf to individual or small group acts of mugging, robbery, or other "gain" or "control" behaviors, perhaps, he asserts, the protection and enhancement of "rep" becomes less focal. We would posit the opposite. Gardner (1983) has noted in this context, "With few resources available to poor urban young people, a reputation for being tough and a good fighter is one of the only ways to attain status" (p. 27). It is a sad commentary on America's priorities, but we believe that such resources have become even scarcer in the years since Gardner's observation, the potential status-enhancing avenues available to our low-income youths even fewer, and thus the need to seek such enhancement by means designated by the larger society as illegal or inappropriate, including overt aggression, even greater. As Klein and Maxson (1989) observe:

> Gang ethnographers . . . have concluded from extended observations that violent activities among gang members serve important social and psychological

functions in asserting masculinity. Especially among Hispanic gangs, the emphasis on machismo and honor have been seen as legitimating and thus facilitating violent behavior in circumstances that challenge gang members' courage or territory. (p. 203)

Sociopathy. One further gang member characteristic that may be relevant in seeking to understand increased levels of contemporary gang violence is sociopathy. The sociopath has been variously described as an individual who (a) is aggressive, reckless, cruel to others, impulsive, manipulative, superficial, callous, irresponsible, cunning, and self-assured (Magdid & McKelvey, 1987); (b) fails to learn by experience, is unable to form meaningful relationships, is chronically antisocial, is unresponsive to punishment, is unable to experience guilt, is self-centered, and lacks a moral sense (Gray & Hutchison, 1964); (c) is unreliable, untruthful, shameless, shows poor judgment, and is highly egocentric (Cleckly, 1964); (d) is unable to show empathy or genuine concern for others, manipulates others toward satisfying his or her own needs, and shows a glib sophistication and superficial sincerity (Hare, 1970); (e) is loveless and guiltless (McCord & McCord, 1964); and (f) shows a particular deficiency in perspective taking or ability to take the role of other persons (Gough, 1948). In 1967 Yablonsky asserted that "the violent gang structure recruits its participants from the more sociopathic youths living in the disorganized slum community" (p. 189). He adds that:

The selection of violence by the sociopathic youth in his adjustment process is not difficult to understand. Violent behavior requires limited training, personal ability, or even physical strength. Because violence is a demonstration of easily achieved power, it becomes the paramount value of the gang. (p. 199)

Reuterman (1975) has similarly observed that "adolescent residents of slum areas who exhibit these traits tend to constitute the membership of violent gangs" (p. 41). If Fahlberg (1979), Magdid and McKelvey (1987), and Rutter (1980) are correct in their contention that early childhood failures of bonding and attachment lie importantly at the roots of such sociopathy, and that societal conditions in America of the 1980s and 1990s are promotive of such failure, then there may now exist an increased likelihood of sociopathic individuals developing. We refer in particular here to the several manifestations of dysfunctional family life currently apparent:

Because of necessity or desire, more and more mothers are returning to work, many just weeks after the birth of their babies. Parents need to know that this may be putting their children at risk for unattachment. Other factors can contribute to faulty infant attachment: high divorce rates, day care problems, lack of a national parent leave policy, epidemic teenage pregnancies, too-late adoptions, [and] the foster care system. (Magdid & McKelvey, 1987, p. 4)

We wish to avoid circularity here. If sociopathic individuals tend to behave aggressively, and more aggression by gang youths seems apparent, we do not by any means necessarily thus have evidence that sociopathy has itself increased. However, we are asserting, given the apparently increased presence of the conditions held to give rise to sociopathic youths, such is not an improbable speculation. Yablonsky (1967) has often been criticized in the academic literature on gangs for purportedly holding that most gang youths and most gang violence have sociopathic roots. We are less declarative and more speculative here. It may be, we wonder, that his observations fit the contemporary American gang even better than the gang youths Yablonsky observed earlier and, some hold, (mis)described.

Immediate Provocations

We have examined both the contextual features (drugs, territory, weapons) and youth characteristics (number, age, honor, sociopathy) that may collectively function as the distal explanations of heightened gang violence in contemporary America. What of its proximal or immediate causes? What are the common provocations or triggers that spark the fuse? No doubt triggers change with culture, time, and place, but the following list from the New York City Youth Board, dated 1960, appears remarkably current. The reader should note that, not unlike the contextual versus youth causal dichotomy we have employed in this chapter, the Youth Board separately identified "exterior" and "interior" provocations:

Exterior Provocations	*Interior Provocations*
Bad looks	Leader power needs
Rumors	Compensation for inadequate self-esteem
Territorial boundary disputes	Acting-out to convince self of potency
Disputes over girls	Acting-out to obtain group affection
Out-of-neighborhood parties	Acting-out to retaliate against fantasized
Drinking	aggression
Narcotics	

Ethnic Tensions

These are, of course, but a sampling of possible provocations to aggression. Moore, Garcia, Garcia, Cerda, and Valencia (1978) have demonstrated that gang youths are not infrequently hypervigilant in their attention to possible slights, and Dodge and Murphy (1984) have shown that such attention often leads to misperceptions of hostile intent and related misinterpretations of neutral events. As the New York City Youth Board (1960) observes:

> The possibilities [for provocation] are almost limitless since the act itself in many cases is relatively unimportant, but rather is seen in a total context of the past, the present, and the future. Further, the act is seen in a total context of its stated, implied, and imagined meanings, all of which are subject to distortion by the groups, individuals, and the gangs. (p. 69)

It is clear from the review presented in this chapter that gang violence in the United States is substantial and growing. Its multisource causality, its multiplicity of expressions, and its multicultural array of perpetrators all make more daunting the hope of successful intervention. In the chapters that follow, we will first consider the stream of past intervention efforts, and what lessons may be drawn from their successes and failures. We will then turn to a full examination of our own entry in this long series, Aggression Replacement Training, an intervention especially focused upon the gang violence forms and levels considered in the present chapter.

Note

1. Vigil (1988) suggests that fighting with rival gangs is most common among gang members still in their early adolescence, that is, still in their reputation-acquiring stage. Later adolescents, he proposes, are more likely to be initiators of gain-associated criminal activities.

II

Gang Intervention

3

An Historical Review

As we suggested in the preceding chapter, juvenile gangs in the early decades of the 20th century, though at times involved in vandalism, fighting, theft, or other antisocial or delinquent acts, purportedly had an almost adventurously playful, benign quality to them (Furfey, 1926; Puffer, 1912; Sheldon, 1949). Or at least such a quaint perception *seems* to be the case from the highly violent gang perspective of the 1990s. Thrasher (1963) observed during that earlier period:

> The quest for new experience seems to be particularly insistent in the adolescent, who finds in the gang the desired escape from, or compensation for, monotony. The gang actively promotes such highly agreeable activities as rough-house, movement and change, games and gambling, predatory activities, seeing thrillers in the movies, sports, imaginative play, roaming and roving, exploration, and camping and hiking. (p. 68)

Though Thrasher and others, anticipating the era of "opportunities provision"—the primary solution to ganging promoted in the 1960s and 1970s—urged social intervention in such "underlying conditions as inadequate family life, poverty, deteriorating neighborhoods, and ineffective religion, education, and recreation" (Thrasher, 1963, p. 339), relatively little such intervention was systematically provided. Police intervention was sometimes necessary, and employed, but more generally the relatively low number of youth gangs in America and the low level of both gang youths' criminality and, especially, violence during these early years yielded but minor concern directed toward formulating gang-oriented strategies and procedures for effective intervention.

As the century progressed and the negative societal conditions apparently generative of youth gang formation spread and grew, so too did both the absolute number of gangs in America and their predatory and conflict-causing quality. Their junior, subsidiary, or ancillary role vis-à-vis adult criminal gangs during the Depression years was, by mid century, increasingly supplanted by juvenile gang-initiated theft, vandalism, and fighting. The latter, though paling in comparison to the considerably more virulent gang violence levels of today, nevertheless aroused sufficient community concern that the search for effective means for intervention became especially active and eventually crystallized in the widespread use of what came to be known as detached workers.

Detached Worker Programs

Two of the major figures in gang intervention programming and evaluation during the past several decades, Irving Spergel of the University of Chicago and Malcolm Klein of the University of Southern California, each contributed importantly to the origination and implementation of the detached worker approach. Their respective views defining its nature and substance are of interest.

According to Spergel (1965):

The practice variously labeled detached work, street club, gang work, area work, extension youth work, corner work, etc., is the systematic effort of an agency worker, through social work or treatment techniques within the neighborhood context, to help a group of young people who are described as delinquent or partially delinquent to achieve a conventional adaptation. (p. 22)

The assumption of youth agencies was that youth gangs were viable or adaptive and could be redirected. Counseling and group activities could be useful in persuading youth gang members to give up unlawful behavior. The small gang group or subgroup was to be the center of attention of the street worker. (p. 145)

Klein (1971) defines this approach further:

Detached work programs are grounded in one basic proposition: Because gang members do not ordinarily respond well to standard agency walls, it is necessary to take the programs to the gangs. Around this simple base of a worker reaching out to his client, other programmatic thrusts then take form—club meetings, sports activities, tutoring, and remedial reading projects,

leadership training, family counseling, casework, employment training, job
finding, and so on. In addition, a community organization component is
often built into the program . . . The primary change mechanism is the rap-
port established between worker and gang members. (p. 46)

Detached work programs grew from an historical context reaching back to
the mid-19th century, in which charity and church groups—as well as Boy
Scouts, Boys' Clubs, YMCAs and settlement houses—sought to establish
relationships with and programs for urban youths in trouble or at risk for
some. Thrasher spoke of such efforts in 1927, and the Chicago Area Projects
of the 1930s (Kobrin, 1959) provided much of the procedural prototype for
the youth outreach, detached work programs that emerged in force in the
1950s and 1960s. And blossom they did. In the fertile context of the social
action movements of mid-century America, many U.S. cities developed and
put such programming in place. Their goals were diverse and ambitious. The
Street Club Project, one of the early programs of the New York City Youth
Board during the period, aspired to provide:

Group work and recreation services to youngsters previously unable to use
the traditional, existing facilities; the opportunity to make referrals of gang
members for necessary treatment . . . the provision of assistance and guidance in the vocational area; and . . . the education of the community to the
fact that . . . members of fighting gangs can be redirected into constructive,
positive paths. (The New York City Youth Board, 1960, p. 7)

At a more general level, this, and many of the detached work programs
that soon followed, also held as their broad goals the reduction of antisocial
behavior; friendlier relations with other street gangs, increased participation
of a democratic nature within the gang; increased responsibility for self-
direction among individual gang members, as well as their improved social
and personal adjustment; and better relations with the larger community of
which the gang was a part.
    As the movement evolved, most detached work programs placed primary
emphasis on value transformation, a rechanneling of the youths' beliefs and
attitudes—and consequently, they hoped, their behavior—in less antisocial
and more prosocial directions. Some programs incorporated components of
opportunities provision (Maxson & Klein, 1983), which years later was to supplant values transformation as the major thrust of gang intervention programming. Others, responding to the many intra-individual, gang, and community
forces that serve to maintain antisocial behavior, had more modest aspirations

and hoped detached work efforts would "hold the line with the individual delinquent . . . until normal processes of maturation take over" (Spergel, 1965, p. 43). As the use of detached work programs continued and implementers developed a further sense of what such efforts might and might not appropriately aspire to accomplish, goal planning became both more refined and more complex. Spergel (1965), for example, described the purposes of detached work programming with delinquent gangs as fourfold:

1. *Control.* To saturate an area with detached work services, offering them to all of the gangs in conflict in the area. In addition to the services, and their consequences thus provided, such saturation of effort yields surveillance and control opportunities which themselves may be conflict-reducing.

2. *Treatment.* To the degree that the antisocial behavior of delinquent gang members is viewed as a resultant, at least in part, of psychological disturbance, successful counseling or therapeutic intervention becomes an appropriate goal for the detached worker. In the 1950s and 1960s, such intervention rested largely on psychoanalytic notions, and was often operationalized by expressive/cathartic interactions aimed at anxiety reduction and the development of more effective personal controls.

3. *Opportunity Provision.* This class of program goals responds to the limited access to and use of educational, employment, and recreational resources often characteristic of delinquent gang youths. Programming, in this view, ought to aspire both to develop and make available such resources, and aid the youths in making use of them.

4. *Value Change.* Via a variety of means, this goal—as noted above— seeks a reorientation or rechanneling of values from antisocial to prosocial, both in the youths themselves and in the adults and organizations in the community—whose norms may be supportive of delinquent, criminal behavior and beliefs.

As observed earlier, several detached worker programs were initiated across the United States: in New York City, Boston, Chicago, Los Angeles, San Francisco, El Paso, and elsewhere. Spergel (1965) has provided the following comprehensive and more or less sequential organization of their (collective) implementation procedures.

1. *Introduction.* Via self-introduction, introduction by a previous worker or by a member of the community, worker and gang meet. The youths' initial response will be a function in part of whether they perceive him as being in a police-like control role; in a social agency, perhaps welfare worker role; or accurately for the role(s) he intends to enact. And, if he is perceived accurately, youth response may vary according to whether "having a worker" is seen as status-enhancing (the community sees us as bad enough to need one), or status-diminishing (preferring to avoid the delinquent label).

2. *Observation and Orientation.* This is the structuring stage of the youth-worker relationship. The worker, capitalizing on one major advantage of being detached from agency to street, begins to observe his target youths in their natural, neighborhood contexts. As opportunities arise or can be created, by word and deed he begins to orient both the youths and significant others (parents, community figures, and so on) to his intended and possible roles and functions.

3. *Meeting Group Tests.* Gang members test and retest the worker, and as part of such testing may display suspicion, ostracism, verbal abuse, and even physical aggression. Spergel (1965) comments:

> Testing takes many forms. For example, at first the youngsters may deliberately fabricate stories of fights or planned criminal activities, requests for help with jobs or problems at school. They are interested mainly in the way he responds to hypothetical situations. . . . The worker is also tested in a very personal way. The group wants to know why he is a street worker and what his personal ambitions are. . . . The group wants to know how far they can push him and in what way they can make him angry. (pp. 76-77)

4. *Assisting the Group to Solve a Problem.* The initial testing ends, and the worker-youth relationship may be said to have been established, suggests Spergel (1965), when the worker assists the group in dealing successfully with a problem that the group sees as significant: "Helping to solve a problem may be as simple as teaching the members how to shoot a basket, how to conduct a dance, or helping youngsters transfer from one school to another" (p. 79).

5. *Dealing With a Sense of Deprivation.* An early and often continuing task for the worker is helping ameliorate the youth's sense of estrangement from his community, perhaps his family, and from others who play a significant role in his life. Gang youths often pessimistically fear further deprivation including, later on, loss of the worker. The emotional climate such a sense

may create can substantially influence both the tone of worker-youth interactions and the likelihood of their outcomes being positive.

6. *Setting Appropriate Standards.* The overriding purpose of detached
work programs, it will be recalled, is to assist gang youth in developing prosocial values and behavior, and in relinquishing antisocial norms and actions.
The behavior and perceived values of significant adults with whom the youths
interact looms large in this challenging, revisionary effort:

> The worker who is warm and friendly, who has gained the respect and admi-
> ration of group members, may be used as a role model. His behavior, atti-
> tudes, and beliefs may become their standards . . . changes in certain pat-
> terns of behavior occur in a generalized, nonplanned way, because of the
> worker's positive relationship with the members. (Spergel, 1965, p. 84)

7. *Decision Making.* In the belief that it ultimately increases both a sense
of satisfaction in the youth, and the level of his conventional behavior, a
democratic decision-making process is strongly encouraged by the worker.
As a component of this effort, the worker urges maximum group responsibility in the control of its own acting-out behavior.

8. *Advice and Normative Controls.* These are straightforward, instruc-
tional communications from worker to youth. On occasion, these communications may go beyond mere advice and admonitions regarding the consequences of planned delinquent behavior, and the value of conformity to more
conventional norms and actions.

9. *Compelling Conformity to Conventional Standards.* Under extreme
circumstances, such as when the worker or someone else is under direct
threat of violence, the worker may have to compel behavioral compliance,
either through his own actions, with the aid of other staff, or by seeking the
assistance of the police.

10. *Other Worker-Initiated Procedures.* Depending upon an almost lim-
itless array of gang member and significant other behaviors, and environmental events, the detached worker may be called upon to implement an
exceedingly broad range of additional procedures and services—planning
and supervising diverse gang programming, contriving circumstances that
minimize the possibility of inter-gang fighting, encouraging the gang's segmen-
tation into conventional and delinquent subgroups when such a polarization
naturally emerges and cannot be reconciled, providing direct instruction

in conventional behaviors (e.g., what to say, when, to whom), and much, much more.[1]

Given this diverse, demanding, and multifaceted array of procedural components to the job of detached worker, it is no wonder that qualifications for such persons have been described, in an article by Fox (1985), aptly titled "Mission Impossible?" as: "Dedicated, abundant energy, a sense of fun, good and quick intelligence, courage, inventiveness, ability to relate to suspicious teenagers, a degree of comfort with authority, and a firm set of values rooted in his own experience, all seem essential" (p. 26).

Four of the detached worker programs thus operationalized are particularly relevant for our further consideration here, since with one exception each was formally and systematically evaluated for its effectiveness or, if left unevaluated (i.e., the New York City Youth Board Project), served nonetheless as a springboard shaping the nature of other such programs. The Roxbury Project (Miller, 1970) was evaluated using a variety of effectiveness criteria and a series of comparison groups. Results on several intermediate criteria were favorable—worker relationships with gangs were established; recreational, educational, and occupational interests were stimulated. However, on the Project's ultimate criterion, "inhibition of law-violating or morally-disapproved behavior" (Quicker, 1983a), no significant between-condition differences emerged. The Chicago Youth Development Project (Mattick & Caplan, 1962) was yet another apparent outcome failure on delinquency-reduction criteria. Results indicated that an intensive worker-youth relationship was not, as had been predicted, positively related to a prosocial outcome. In fact, the youths who claimed to be closest to their detached workers were most in trouble with the police. The Los Angeles Group Guidance Project (Klein, 1968b) was also fully evaluated, and it too proved to be a seemingly inadequate approach to rechanneling the values and behavior of delinquent gang youths. Gang member delinquency actually increased over the course of the Project's life, and did so especially for those youths who received the fullest worker attention.

It is not often the case in social science research that such a clear confluence of results (positive or negative) emerges, and thus it is not surprising that gang researchers more or less unanimously concluded that the detached work approach ought not be pursued further. Klein (1968b), in particular, urged this step, claiming that the consistently negative results were largely an outcome of the manner in which detached work programming attended primarily to the gang as a group, and less to its individual members, thus enhancing gang cohesiveness, perpetuating and not rechanneling the gang, and drawing new recruits to its membership. Klein's (1968b) programmatic response to these conclusions, the more individually oriented, cohesiveness-reducing, gangbusting Ladino Hills Project—which did succeed in reducing the absolute level of delinquency (mostly because the gangs' sizes shrunk)— seemed to him and others to be the evidential nail in the detached work program's coffin.

Negative evidence notwithstanding, there is more to the evaluation story to be told. It is our belief that all of the detached work programs described above suffer from one, and typically several, failures of implementation. In each instance, both implementation plans and evaluation procedures seem adequate, but not the manner in which worker activities were actually conducted. If this is the case, program effectiveness remains indeterminate, and conclusions regarding outcome efficacy must be suspended. There are five reasons for taking this position: (a) failure of program integrity, (b) failure of program intensity, (c) absence of techniques relevant to delinquency reduction, (d) failure of program prescriptiveness, and (e) failure of program comprehensiveness. The sections that follow will elaborate upon these evaluative shortfalls because they, and the conclusion of indeterminacy of program effectiveness, apply not only to detached work gang programming but also to a number of other approaches to gang intervention. We also wish to discuss these implementation shortcomings here because we have sought to eliminate, or at least minimize, their existence in our own, ART, gang intervention and evaluation effort.

Program Integrity

Program integrity refers to the degree to which the intervention as actually implemented corresponded to or followed the intervention program as planned. As we noted in our New York State Juvenile Gang Taskforce Report (New York State Division for Youth, 1990):

> If youth at risk of gang involvement are to be served adequately, it is critical that programs developed be actually implemented according to planned program procedures. Too often, mostly as a result of too few personnel or inadequate funding, programs of apparent substantial potential are actually implemented inadequately. (p. 44)

Failure of program integrity, as thus defined, appears to have been a not infrequent characteristic of the detached work programs we have examined. The New York State Youth Board Project, according to Gannon (1965), repeatedly suffered from "high staff turnover," "monumental red tape," "low staff morale," "worker role confusion," and a number of other, kindred threats to program integrity. In the Chicago Youth Development Project, "the workers found their jobs so demanding [that] they tend to swallow up the whole life of the person holding them" (Quicker, 1983a). Even more directly bearing on intervention plan/intervention implementation correspondence, Klein (1968b) notes with regard to the Group Guidance Project that its worker counseling policy component was "confused"; that its planned parent groups component was largely nonexistent; that its psychiatric intervention component was "inflexible"; and that its program integrity–promoting supervisory plan was severely inadequate in its actual implementation. With regard to this last, responding to the fact that program supervisors wound up spending less than 30 minutes per worker per week in field supervision and observation, Klein (1968b) comments:

> Action in the street scene means, almost inevitably, lower levels of line supervision. . . . For the researcher, this supervisorial gap poses serious problems of data validity, discrepant views of the action, feedback mechanics, and proper implementation of program . . . procedures. In other words, there is little control, and certainly less than is found in most action-research settings. (p. 235)

Program Intensity

Program intensity refers to the intensity with which an intervention is delivered, that is, its amount, level, or dosage. Again excerpting our own recent observation on this important intervention feature:

> In general, it will be the case that "the more the better," whether referring to amount of youth contact with the interveners; amount of counseling time, recreational time or job skills training time; or amount of family or community involvement in programming for youth. (New York State Division for Youth, 1990, p. 45)

On this criterion of project adequacy, the detached work programs of concern here do not do well. Worker-youth ratios were an acceptable 1 to 29 in the Roxbury Project, an unacceptable 1 to 78 in the New York City Youth Board

Program, and a quite impossible 1 to 92 in the Chicago Youth Development Project. Such disproportionate caseloads usually meant that youths were rarely worked with individually, and almost always in groups. As Mulvihill, Tumin, and Curtis (1969) observe:

> How would a rational worker go about meeting and maintaining rapport with as many as a hundred youngsters much of whose lives are street oriented? Being on the street himself is not sufficient; too many boys are missed that way. The worker has little choice but to encourage group gatherings. (p. 1455)

These "gatherings," as Dumpson (1949) noted in connection with the New York City Youth Board Project, can mean dealing with as many as 50 youths at a time.

Klein's (1968b) Group Guidance Project intensity data are most telling on this topic. The Project's detached workers, it seems, were in reality only partly detached. They spent 25% to 50% of their time (on average 38%, or about two fifths) in the Project office, and a considerable amount of time (average 25%) alone (traveling, "hanging around" gathering spots). Thus, almost two thirds of their typical working day was not spent with project youths. He pointedly comments:

> Whether one looks at this as an hour and a half a day, a day a week, or ten weeks out of a year, this is a fascinating piece of information. Gang workers in this project spent one-fifth of their time with gang members. . . . With 50 to 100 gang members in the neighborhood, and eight hours a week spent in contact with them, how much impact can reasonably be expected? It may be like squeezing blood out of a turnip to think that an average of five minutes per week per boy could somehow result in a reduction of delinquent behavior. (p. 163)

So much for intervention intensity!

Absence of Delinquency-Relevant Techniques

Well-designed evaluations of intervention programs often include both proximal and distal measures of the intervention's effectiveness. The former are tied directly to the contents of the intervention—if remedial reading was the intervention, has the youth's reading level advanced; if social skills training was provided, is he more socially skilled; and if employment interviewee behaviors were taught, how does he actually behave in a mock or real interview?

Distal, or more derivative outcome measures, are criteria on which the youth may improve, usually if and only if prior improvement on the proximal or more immediate criterion of change has first taken place. Thus, grade point average might well be a distal criterion of intervention effectiveness in a remedial reading intervention employing the proximal criterion of change in reading level. Level of self-esteem might similarly be the derivative criterion in a social skills intervention; and actual job attainment could be the distal measure in the instance of employment interviewee training. In the evaluation of detached work programs, a variety of appropriate proximal measures has been employed, but its criterion of distal effectiveness (and raison d'etre) has consistently been change in delinquent behavior. Combined outcome evidence is fairly supportive of the proximal effectiveness of detached work but, as noted earlier, consistently unsupportive of its distal effectiveness thus defined.

Though the potency of available, *delinquency-altering* techniques has improved since the era of detached work programming, it is even now still largely inappropriate to predict that an (any) intervention targeted to behavior, attitude, or value A will be so potent that, in addition to changing A, it will also impact significantly on (derivative criterion) B. Our available interventions in the realm of delinquency intervention are simply not that powerful. Klein (1968b), in examining the outcome of his Group Guidance Project, comments in this regard:

> Another weakness derives from the general lack of knowledge in the entire field of delinquency prevention, and the worker is the unfortunate bearer of this burden. I refer here to the lack of specific techniques for dealing with specific forms of delinquent behavior. An exception is the control of gang fighting in which worker visibility, the provision of face saving alternatives, and truce meetings are accepted procedures for avoiding territorial raids and retaliations. Unfortunately, few techniques exist that are comparably effective with theft, rape, malicious mischief, auto theft, truancy, and so on. This lack of specific behavior related techniques forces the worker to fall back upon general intervention procedures such as individual or family counseling, group activities, job development, and so on, procedures which at best have only an indirect relationship to delinquency producing situations. (p. 150)

Thus, in the Group Guidance Project, a diverse array of 241 (usually group) activities were conducted over the 2.5 years of the program's life, an average of two activities per week. In spite of their diversity, their contents were such that the evaluators concluded: "It was clear from our observations that the special activities were seldom used directly . . . for delinquency prevention. Any major positive impact on delinquency would have to be indirect, through self-discovered lessons about fair play, the value of prosocial activity, and so on" (Klein, 1968b, p. 169).

These absence-of-technique conclusions, in addition to engendering our admiration of Klein and his research team for both their research acumen and remarkable candor, ought, we hope, be taken as both insight and a stimulus: insight regarding the need for more direct and potent delinquency interventions; stimulus for the effort to produce same.

Program Prescriptiveness

As delinquency-relevant interventions are developed and become available, and are implemented with both integrity to plan and intensity of dosage, they must also be applied prescriptively. The detached work programs under consideration here, as is true of the vast majority of delinquency intervention programming of whatever kind, were not employed in a differential, tailored, individualized, or prescriptive manner. We believe the success of interventions such as detached work is likely to be substantially enhanced to the degree that the worker's techniques (and worker characteristics) are propitiously matched with qualities of the participating youth. Valuable beginning leads in this regard already exist, including notions urging different approaches to core versus marginal gang members (Yablonsky, 1967); leaders versus followers (Needle & Stapleton, 1982); to older versus younger youths (Spergel et al., 1989); to youths from theft, conflict, or racket subcultures (Spergel et al., 1989); to gang youths classified by both degree of aggressiveness and degree of gang involvement (Klein, 1968a); to youths classified as clique leaders, cohesiveness builders, recruits, and best bets (Klein, 1968a); or in response to diverse worker qualities. The latter, an especially ignored but, we believe, an especially outcome-relevant prescriptive ingredient, is captured well by Spergel et al.:

> A key objective should be to match the skills of the worker optimally with the needs of the group. For example, the worker who is particularly effective in setting limits should be assigned to a group which has great difficulty in controlling its aggressive impulses; a worker who is skilled at individual and group treatment should work with a group requiring therapeutic help; a worker who is talented at opening up and developing community resources for socioeconomically deprived youths should be assigned to a group needing access to appropriate opportunities. (p. 29)

In general, we are urging that the proper, if complex, prescriptive question to be addressed is "Which types of youths in which types of gangs being serviced by which types of detached workers will yield which types of pro-social outcomes?"

Program Comprehensiveness

It was the intent of all of the detached work programs considered here to provide not only the main intervention components associated with worker-youth relationships, but also comprehensive, multilevel programming, to both the youth and the systems of which he was a part. Thus, the New York City Youth Board Project (1960) commented:

It has been asked whether it is most productive to work with the group, with the individual in the group, or with the community itself, and through changes in the community, bring about changes in the group. Traditionally the work of the Street Club Project has been focussed on all three: the group, the neighborhood and the individual members themselves. This stems from our conviction that delinquency is caused by a multiplicity of factors—both individual and social—and that an effective approach to the problem should incorporate both of these areas. (p. 118)

Given the long, formative, and frequently antisocially oriented life history of many gang youths, and their levels of contemporary reinforcement for continuing to engage in antisocial behavior, this multipronged intervention aspiration seems most appropriate. Yet detached workers in the programs implemented were overworked, undertrained, and had few resources at their disposal. Most of what was available to them was youth-oriented in its substance and target, not system-oriented. Thus, rather than intervention comprehensiveness, what actually emerged

targeted specific gangs and gang youth. It was not integrated into other service or community development approaches occurring at the same time. It concentrated on the development of worker-gang member relationships and recreational and group activities in somewhat isolated terms. It was a fairly unidimensional approach. (Klein, 1968b, p. 52)

These several intervention implementation shortfalls—regarding integrity to plan, intensity of administration, absence of delinquency-relevant techniques, prescriptiveness of implementation, and comprehensiveness of program—

characterize not only the four detached work projects primarily focused upon in this chapter, but also other, similar programs: El Paso (Quicker, 1983a), the YMCA Project in Chicago (Spergel et al., 1989), San Francisco's Youth for Service Project (Klein, 1968b), and others. Given these implementation realities, our examination of the nature and efficacy of detached work programming must conclude: "We would hold the relevant evidence, instead of being interpreted as proof of lack of effectiveness, should more parsimoniously be viewed as indeterminate, generally neither adding to nor detracting from a conclusion of effectiveness or ineffectiveness" (Goldstein, 1990).

Opportunities Provision Programs

Gang intervention programming, whatever its major thrust, has always contained at least some attention to enhancing the extra-gang opportunity structure available to such youths. But in some eras, it has been decidedly minor attention. During the decades of detached work programming, for example, primary programming emphasis was consistently placed on the worker-youth relationship and attempts to alter youth behavior by gang reorientation and value transformation, with relatively little effort directed at *system* change, for example, the enhancement of work, school, or family opportunity. Awareness of the incompleteness or asymmetry of this perspective, coupled with the purported gang-cohesiveness and delinquency-enhancing effects of detached work programming—all in a context of increased general promotion in the United States of diverse social legislation—were among the major antecedents, and stimulants of the birth and growth of the phase of gang work that followed, namely opportunities provision. Spergel et al. (1989) describe this strategy as:

> A series of large scale social resource infusions and efforts to change institutional structures, including schools, job opportunities, political employment . . . in the solution not only of delinquency, but poverty itself. Youth work strategies were regarded as insufficient. Structural strain, lack of resources, and relative deprivation were the key ideas which explained delinquency, including youth gang behavior. The structures of social and economic means rather than the behavior of gangs and individual youth had to be modified. (p. 147)

The proposed relevance of this strategy to gang youth in particular is captured well by Morales (1981): "The gang is a symptom of certain noxious conditions found in society. These conditions often include low wages, unemployment, lack of recreational opportunities, inadequate schools, poor health, deteriorated housing and other factors contributing to urban decay and slums" (p. 4).

Quicker (1983b) echoed this perspective, and stressed even more the need for opportunity provision:

> The development of gangs stems primarily from environmental causes. It appears that the legitimate opportunity system is closed to most lower class boys who, having internalized middle class norms of success, are frustrated by their inability to succeed in socially prescribed ways. Joining with other boys, similarly frustrated, they form gangs which provide some of them access to that illegitimate opportunity system (an illegal economy) where they are able at least partially to realize their aspirations. (p. 11)

So too did Klein (1968b), in joint response to the apparent failure of his detached work Group Guidance Project and the subsequent greater success of his opportunities-oriented Ladino Hill Project. He comments:

> One of the difficulties encountered by many past programs stems from the enormous complexity of the gang problem. It has been assumed that a problem deriving its existence from a multitude of sources (family, community, economic deprivation, individual deficiencies, etc.) must be dealt with on all levels. Yet most gang programs have been of the detached worker variety, a form of intervention for which this multilevel approach is inefficient at best, and in reality almost impossible. Detached workers can have relatively little impact on individual character disorders or psychological deficiencies, family relationships, poverty, educational and employment disadvantages, community disorganization and apathy, and so on. (p. 238)

The need for provision of utilitarian and esteem-enhancing opportunity, of course, was apparent as far back as Thrasher's (1927) work and earlier. What was different in the late 1960s and 1970s was America's willingness to respond to such beliefs with a broad programmatic effort. And indeed, many dozens of varied opportunity-providing programs followed. A sampler of those oriented in particular to gang youths includes Mobilization for Youth's (Cloward & Ohlin, 1960; Miller, 1974) provision of vocational guidance and the opportunity to gain small business work experience; Spergel's (1965) street gang project consisting in part of substantial involvement with gang members' families, employers and employment services, public school personnel, and a variety of youth agencies; Klein's (1968b) Ladino Hills

Project, whose "resource workers" (rather than "detached workers") sought to provide participating gang youth employment, improved school opportunities, and enhanced access to recreational, health, and welfare resources; Baca's (1988) Citywide Mural Project; the 1973 New York Police Probation Diversion Project (Gardner, 1983) providing special education and substance abuse prevention programming; Krisberg's (1974) Urban Leadership Training Program, which attempted to train gang leaders for careers in community service; DeLeon's (1977) corporation- and police-initiated scouting troops; Haire's (1979) Rampart gang study mobilizing a unified school district to provide expanded educational opportunities; the Hire a Gang Leader program (Amandes, 1979), teaching an array of job-seeking and job-keeping skills and providing actual employment opportunities; the Ocean Township Youth Volunteer Corps (Torchia, 1980), which offered both community service and diverse recreational possibilities to adjudicated gang youth; Sweeney's (1981) job, school and neighborhood-oriented Community Gang Service Project; Willman and Snortum's (1982) Project New Pride and Gang Employment Programs, both of which emphasized job training and employment opportunity programming, as did Falaka's House of Umoja (Gardner, 1983); Project Say (Save-A-Youth), developed by Willis-Kistler (1988), offering a full array of family, school, and recreational opportunities; Thompson and Jason's (1988) school and after-school Project BUILD (Broader Urban Involvement and Leadership Development); the employment-oriented Community Access Team (California Youth Gang Task Force, 1981); Youth Enterprises of Long Beach (Quicker, 1983a) and SEY Yes (Quicker, 1983a) programs; the school-oriented GREAT (Gang Resistance and Training) (Los Angeles Unified School District, 1989), PREP (Preparation through Responsive Education) (Filipczak, Friedman, & Reese, 1979), and Gangs Network (college-option generating) (Needle & Stapleton, 1982) programs; and the family-oriented Family and School Consultation Project (Stuart, Jayaratne, & Tripoldi, 1976) and Aggression Replacement Training Project (Goldstein, Glick, Irwin, Pask-McCartney, & Rubama, 1989) programs.

Prescriptive Evaluation

With very few exceptions (e.g., Klein, 1968b; Thompson & Jason, 1988), opportunities provision gang programming has not been systematically evaluated. We do not know with any substantial degree of evaluative rigor either whether or the degree to which gang youths in general, or particular gang subgroups, accept or seek the diverse opportunities provided, nor whether they benefit in either proximal, opportunity-specific ways, or more distally in terms of termination of gang membership, delinquency reduction, or future life path. There is no shortage of affirming impressionistic and anecdotal support—including a major 45-city survey of both law enforcement and non-law enforcement agency views on the effectiveness of opportunity-provision and other gang intervention approaches (Spergel et al., 1989)—but its heuristic value is clearly limited, especially its value for determination of future programming. Klein's (1968b) Ladino Hills Project is an important exception; its careful evaluation sets a standard to be aspired to. Especially noteworthy is its prescriptive feature, a systematic effort to develop a typology of gang youths whose categories are differentially responsive to different patterns of opportunities provision (and other) programming. We have sought to make a strong case for such a strategy elsewhere in this book, and will not repeat it here save to note that Klein's (1968b) initial success in this attempt well deserves replication and elaboration by others. His gang youth categories— Clique Leaders, Cohesiveness Builders, Recruits, and Best Bets—make both intuitive and empirical sense.

Utilization and evaluation of the opportunity-provision strategy, regardless of whether implemented prescriptively, would optimally also be responsive to Spergel et al.'s (1989) urging that its success will be more likely when opportunities are offered with sufficient *support* and *organization*. They comment:

A general design for improved living in particularly deprived lower-class areas should be based on three concepts: opportunity, service, and organization. . . . Since the provision of basic social and economic opportunities is not enough, however, a variety of significant social supports, through services, must be developed to insure that the expanded opportunities which become available to the child at school or to the parent through a better job are utilized. Social work, as well as psychological, psychiatric, health, and other community services, must be amply provided to many parents and children so that the basic opportunities are appropriately appreciated and used. . . . Even the provision of expanded opportunities and services may still not be enough to prevent social ills and to rehabilitate problem families and their children. Expanded opportunities and services must be efficiently organized. Too often, problem youngsters and their families are shunted from agency to agency . . . many programs in deprived neighborhoods lack quality, imagination, and flexibility. Untrained and poorly supervised personnel are presented with intolerably heavy and difficulty assignments which they cannot handle effectively. Stereotyped and inferior practices at schools and agencies are little better than no teaching at all. (pp. 173-174)

The effectiveness of opportunities provision, it is thus urged, is a joint resultant of the opportunities provided; the manner in which they are delivered; and their coordination, organization, or interrelatedness.

Deterrence/Incarceration Programs

As the 1970s drew to a close, America got tough. As described in Chapter 2, a combination of the heavy influx of drugs, growing levels of violence, purported failure of rehabilitative programming, and the rise of political and judicial conservatism all compounded to usher in the era of deterrence/ incarceration and begin ushering out the provision of social, economic, and educational opportunity. Opportunity provision is not gone, but it is much, much less frequently the centerpiece of gang intervention programming. Social control—surveillance, deterrence, arrest, prosecution, incarceration—has largely replaced social infusion as America's preeminent approach to gang youth:

> A philosophy of increased social opportunity was replaced by growing conservatism. The gang was viewed as evil, a collecting place for sociopaths who were beyond the capacity of most social institutions to redirect or rehabilitate them. Protection of the community became the key goal. (Spergel et al., 1989, p. 148)

The deterrence/incarceration strategy came to guide the gang-relevant behavior not only of law enforcement personnel but also of others. In Philadelphia's Crisis Intervention Network program, in Los Angeles' Community Youth Gang Services, and in the other similar gang crisis intervention programs that sprang up across America, the resource worker, who himself had replaced the detached worker, was in turn replaced by the surveillance/ deterrence worker. Working out of radio-dispatched automobiles, and assigned to geographical areas rather than to specific gangs, such surveillance/ deterrence workers responded to crises, their focus on rumor control, dispute resolution, and, most centrally, violence reduction. Maxson and Klein (1983) capture well the essence of this strategy, as they contrast it with the earlier, value transformation approach:

> The transformation model fostered social group work in the streets with empathic and sympathetic orientations toward gang members as well as acceptance of gang misbehavior as far less of a problem than the alienating response of community residents and officials. By contrast, the deterrence model eschews

an interest in minor gang predations and concentrates on the major ones, especially homicide. The worker is, in essence, part of a dramatically energized community control mechanism, a "firefighter" with a more balanced eye on the consequences as well as the cause of gang violence. Success is measured first in violence reduction, not in group or individual change. (p. 151)

It is, of course, the police and other agents of America's criminal justice system who are the primary implementers of the deterrence/incarceration approach to gang intervention. It is a largely suppressive approach, employing such tactics as surveillance, stakeout, aggressive patrol, intelligence gathering, infiltration, investigation, prosecution, and incarceration. Its spirit is captured well by Hagedorn and Macon (1988): "The basic strategy for coping with gangs remains the iron fist, a strategy that moves the problem from visibility in the community to the invisibility of the prison" (p. 150).

Comprehensive Programs

Indeed, it is a primary responsibility of society's officialdom to protect its citizens. Gang violence in its diverse and often intense forms must be surveilled, deterred, punished. But much more must be done. Gang youths are *our* youths. They are among us now, and even if periodically incarcerated, most will be among us in the future. We deserve protection from their predations, but they deserve, too, opportunity to lead satisfying and contributory lives without resorting to individual or group violence. Punishment may have to be employed, but punishment fails to teach new, alternative means to desired goals. In essence, the implementations of the deterrence/incarceration model may indeed be necessary in today's violence-prone America, but they are far from sufficient. What is needed, and hopefully appears beginning to emerge, is a less unidimensional and more integrative gang intervention model, one with at least the potential to supplant exclusive employment of deterrence/incarceration. We term it "The Comprehensive Model" (similar in spirit and, in large measure, its particulars to Spergel et al.'s "Model B"),[2] one that incorporates and seeks to prescriptively apply major features of detached worker, opportunities provision, and social control programming. It is a multimodal, multilevel strategy requiring substantial resources of diverse types, employed in a coordinated manner for its success to be realized. We have documented elsewhere the manner in which aggressive and antisocial behavior derive from complex causality and, hence, will yield most readily

TABLE 3.1   Comprehensive Gang Intervention Programming

I. Individual-Oriented Interventions
   1. Interpersonal Skills Training
   2. Anger Control
   3. Moral Reasoning Training
   4. Contingency Management
   5. Cognitive Behavioral Interventions

II. System-Oriented Interventions
   6. Family-Based
   7. School-Based
   8. Vocational/Employment
   9. Recreational
   10. Community-Based

III. Criminal Justice Interventions
   11. Police
   12. Prosecutorial
   13. Correctional

when approached with interventions of parallel complexity and targeting (Goldstein, 1983). So, too, for gang aggression and antisocial behavior.

A possible, and we believe likely productive, concretization of a comprehensive gang-intervention strategy is depicted in Table 3.1 We believe that such gang intervention programming, seeking as it must to both decrease and deter the antisocial and promote and encourage the prosocial, ought to strategically enact a "weed and seed" intervention philosophy. For chronically antisocial gang youths, and in particular that small proportion of members who commit a high proportion of violent crimes, criminal justice "weeding" may be the optimal intervention focus—operationalized in Table 3.1 by an array of police, prosecutorial, and correctional interventions. For the fringe member, the wanna-be, the youth not yet heavily committed to aggressive and other antisocial gang-related behaviors, an intervention environment seeded with a rich array of promising individually-oriented and system-oriented interventions seems a most promising strategy. Unfortunately, in contemporary America, in this era of social control, we have weeded heavily and seeded sparingly.

In the chapters that follow, we turn our focus to the intervention central to the present gang-intervention project, Aggression Replacement Training. Its constituent procedures are the first three individual-oriented interventions listed in Table 3.1—interpersonal skills training, anger control, and moral reasoning training. As will be described in Chapter 6, our program was implemented in the context of two inner-city youth agencies, which, along with providing the participating gang members with ART, also offered a broad array of family, school, vocational, and recreational services. Thus, while our explicit focus in the chapters that follow is upon ART, it is clear that both it and the several system-oriented services rendered combine to provide a good first approximation to a sound operational definition of comprehensive gang intervention programming.

This chapter traced the history and development of gang intervention efforts in the United States during the 20th century. Benign neglect of low-level, gang-originated problems gave way in mid-century to the *detached worker* approach. Evaluated as ineffective, though in fact never adequately implemented, it yielded to the *opportunities provision* strategy during the heady, social infusion decades of the 1960s and early 1970s. As America, in turn, grew more conservative in its attitudes toward many social problems in the 1970s and 1980s, so too did it in relation to juvenile gangs. The *deterrence/ incarceration* era, still largely with us in the 1990s, was ushered in. However, there are the beginnings of a new constellation of much of the foregoing, a perhaps more prescriptive and more potent combination of carrot and stick, the *comprehensive* approach to gang intervention. We strongly support this strategy, as it appears more accurately than single-targeted approaches to respond to the multicausal complexity of gang formation and behavior.

Notes

1. Additional detailed descriptions of detached gang work are provided by Bernstein (1964); Crawford, Malamud, and Dumpson (1950); and Fox (1985).

2. Spergel et al. (1989) comment that this model "assumes that the gang problem may be only partially amenable to police suppression. Gang interventions must be defined in broader terms. The youth gang suppression strategy must be incorporated as part of an interagency community collaborative approach which also gives due attention to prevention and social intervention" (p. 173).

4

Aggression Replacement Training
Background and Procedures

Until the early 1970s there existed primarily three major clusters of psychological interventions designed to alter the behavior of aggressive, unhappy, ineffective, or disturbed individuals—psychodynamic/psychoanalytic, humanistic/nondirective, and behavior modification. Each of these diverse orientations found concrete expression in procedures targeted to the group of persons of central concern to the present program, aggressive adolescents—the psychodynamic in psychoanalytically oriented individual psychotherapy (Guttman, 1970), activity group therapy (Slavson, 1964), and the varied array of treatment procedures developed by Redl and Wineman (1957); the humanistic/client centered in the applications to juvenile delinquents (e.g., Truax, Wargo, & Silber, 1966) of the client-centered psychotherapy of Carl Rogers (1957), the alternative educational programs offered by Gold (1978), and the approach to school discipline put forth by Dreikurs, Grunwald, and Pepper (1971); and the behavior modification in a wide variety of the interventions reflecting the systematic use of contingency management, contracting and the training of teachers and parents as behavior change managers (O'Leary, O'Leary, & Becker, 1967; Patterson, Cobb, & Ray, 1973; Walker, 1979). Though each of these intervention philosophies differs from the others in several major respects, one of their significant commonalities is the shared assumption that the targeted client had somewhere within himself, as yet unexpressed, the effective, satisfying, nonaggressive, or healthy behaviors whose expression was among the goals of the intervention. Such latent potentials, in all three approaches, would be realized by the client if the intervener were sufficiently skilled in reducing or removing obstacles to such realization. The psychoanalyst sought to do so by calling forth and interpreting unconscious material blocking progress-relevant awareness. The client-centered therapist, who in particular believed that the potential for change resides within the client, sought to free this potential by providing a warm, empathic, maximally accepting intervention environment. And the behavior modifier, by means of one or more contingency management procedures, attempted to see to it that when the latent desirable behaviors or approximations thereto did occur, the client received contingent reinforcement, thus increasing the probability that these behaviors would recur. Therefore, whether sought by means of interpretation, provision of a positive intervention climate, or by dint of offering contingent reward, all three approaches assumed that somewhere within the individual's repertoire resided the desired, effective goal behaviors.

In the early 1970s an important new intervention approach began to emerge—psychological skill training, an approach resting upon rather different assumptions. Viewing the helpee more in educational, pedagogic terms rather than as a client in need of therapy, the psychological skills trainer assumed he was dealing with an individual lacking, deficient, or at best weak in the skills necessary for effective and satisfying interpersonal and intrapersonal functioning. The task of the skills trainer became, therefore, not interpretation, reflection, or reinforcement, but the active and deliberate teaching of desirable behaviors. Rather than an intervention called psychotherapy, between a patient and psychotherapist, what emerged was training, between a trainee and a psychological skills trainer.

The roots of the psychological skills training movement lie within both education and psychology. The notion of literally seeking to teach desirable behaviors has often, if sporadically, been a significant goal of the American educational establishment. The Character Education Movement of the 1920s and more contemporary Moral Education and Values Clarification programs are but a few of several possible examples. Add to this institutionalized educational interest in skills training, the hundreds of interpersonal and planning skills courses taught in America's more than 2,000 community colleges, and the hundreds of self-help books oriented toward similar skill-enhancement goals that are available to the American public, and it becomes clear that the formal and informal educational establishment in America provided fertile soil and explicit stimulation within which the psychological skills training movement could grow.

Much the same can be said for American psychology, as it too laid the groundwork in its prevailing philosophy and concrete interests for the development of this new movement. The learning process has above all else been the central theoretical and investigative concern of American psychology since the late 19th century. This focal interest also assumed major therapeutic form in the 1950s, as psychotherapy practitioners and researchers alike came to view psychotherapeutic treatment more and more in learning terms. The very healthy and still expanding field of behavior modification grew from this joint learning-clinical focus, and may be appropriately viewed as the immediately preceding context in which psychological skills training came to be developed. In companion with the growth of behavior modification, psychological thinking increasingly shifted from a strict emphasis on remediation to one that was almost equally concerned with prevention, and the bases for this shift included movement away from a medical model concept toward what may most aptly be called a psychoeducational theoretical stance. Both of these thrusts—heightened concern with prevention and a psychoeducational perspective—gave strong added impetus to the viability of the psychological skills training movement.

Perhaps psychology's most direct contribution to psychological skills training came from social learning theory and in particular from the work conducted by and stimulated by Albert Bandura (1973):

> The method that has yielded the most impressive results with diverse problems contains three major components. First, alternative modes of response are repeatedly modeled, preferably by several people who demonstrate how the new style of behavior can be used in dealing with a variety of . . . situations. Second, learners are provided with guidance and ample opportunities to practice the modeled behavior under favorable conditions until they perform it skillfully and spontaneously. The latter procedures are ideally suited for developing new social skills, but they are unlikely to be adopted unless they produce rewarding consequences. Arrangement of success experiences, particularly for initial efforts at behaving differently, constitute the third component in this powerful composite method. . . . Given adequate demonstration, guided practice, and success experiences, this method is almost certain to produce favorable results. (p. 253)

Other events of the 1970s provided still further stimulation for the growth of the skills training movement. The inadequacy of prompting, shaping, and related operant procedures for adding new behaviors to individuals' behavioral repertoires was increasingly apparent. The widespread reliance upon deinstitutionalization, which lay at the heart of the community mental health movement, resulted in the discharge from America's public mental health hospitals of approximately 400,000 persons, the majority of whom were substantially deficient in important daily functioning skills. And it had grown particularly clear that what the American mental health movement had available to offer lower social class clients was grossly inadequate in meeting their psychotherapeutic needs. These factors, that is, relevant supportive research, the incompleteness of operant approaches, large populations of grossly skill-deficient individuals, and the paucity of useful interventions for a large segment of American society—all in the context of historically supportive roots in both education and psychology—came together in our thinking and that of others as demanding a new intervention, something prescriptively responsive to these several needs. Psychological skill training was the answer, and a movement was launched.

Skillstreaming

Our involvement in this movement, a psychological skills-training approach termed Skillstreaming, began in the early 1970s. At that time, and for several years thereafter, our studies were conducted in public mental health hospitals with long-term, highly skill-deficient, chronic patients. As the research program progressed, and demonstrated with regularity successful skill-enhancement effects (Goldstein, 1981), focus shifted from teaching a broad array of interpersonal and daily living skills to adult psychiatric inpatients to a more explicit concern with skill training for aggressive individuals. Trainee groups included spouses engaged in family disputes violent enough to warrant police intervention (Goldstein, Monti, Sardino, & Green, 1979), child-abusing parents (Solomon, 1978; Sturm, 1979), and most especially, overtly aggressive adolescents (Goldstein, Sprafkin, Gershaw, & Klein, 1980).

With regard to adolescent trainees, Skillstreaming has been successful in enhancing such prosocial skills as empathy, negotiation, assertiveness, following instructions, self-control, and perspective taking. Beyond these initial demonstrations that Skillstreaming enhances skill acquisition for such youngsters, these beginning studies also highlighted other aspects of the teaching of prosocial behaviors. Fleming (1976), in an effort to capitalize upon adolescent responsiveness to peer influence, demonstrated that gains in negotiating skill are as great when the Skillstreaming group leader is a respected peer as when the leader is an adult. Litwack (1976), more concerned with the skill-enhancing effect of an adolescent anticipating that he will later serve as a peer leader, showed that such helper role expectation increases that degree of skill acquired. Apparently, when the adolescent expects to teach others a skill, his own level of skill acquisition benefits, a finding clearly relevant to

Reissman's helper therapy principle (1965). Trief (1976) demonstrated that successful use of Skillstreaming to increase perspective-taking skill (i.e., seeing matters from other people's viewpoints) also leads to consequent increases in cooperative behavior. The significant transfer effects both in this study and in the Golden (1975), Litwack (1976), and Raleigh (1977) investigations have been important signposts in planning further research on transfer enhancement in Skillstreaming.

As in earlier efforts with adult trainees, the value of teaching certain skill combinations to adolescents was also examined. Aggression-prone adolescents often get into difficulty when they respond with overt aggression to authority figures with whom they disagree. Golden (1975), responding to this type of event, successfully used Skillstreaming to teach such youngsters resistance-reducing behavior, defined as a combination of reflection of feeling (the authority figure's) and assertiveness (forthright but nonaggressive statement of one's own position). Jennings (1975) was able to use Skillstreaming successfully to train adolescents in several of the verbal skills necessary for satisfactory participation in more traditional, insight-oriented psychotherapy. And Guzzetta (1974) was successful in providing means to help close the gap between adolescents and their parents by using Skillstreaming to teach empathic skills to parents.

The overall conclusions that may justifiably be drawn from these several early empirical evaluations of our work with aggressive adolescent, as well as other trainees, are twofold.

1.   Skill acquisition: Across diverse trainee populations (including aggressive adolescents in urban secondary schools and juvenile detention centers) and target skills, skill acquisition is a reliable training outcome, occurring in better than 90% of Skillstreaming trainees. It is acknowledged that gains demonstrable in the training context are, relatively speaking, rather easily accomplished, given the potency, support, encouragement, and low threat value of trainers and procedures in that context. The more consequential outcome question by far pertains to trainee skill performance in real-world contexts (i.e., skill transfer).

2.   Skill transfer: Across diverse trainee populations, target skills, and applied (real-world) settings, skill transfer occurs with approximately 45% to 50% of Skillstreaming trainees. Goldstein and Kanfer (1979), as well as Karoly and Steffen (1980), have indicated that across several dozen types of psychotherapy involving many different types of psychopathology, the av-

erage transfer rate on follow-up is between 15% and 20% of patients seen. The 45% to 50% rate consequent to Skillstreaming is a significant improvement upon this collective base rate, though it must immediately be underscored that this cumulative average transfer also means that the gains shown by half of the trainees were limited to in-session acquisition. Of special consequence, however, is the consistently clear manner in which skill transfer was a function of the explicit implementation of the laboratory-derived transfer-enhancing techniques discussed later in this chapter.

Interpersonal, aggression-management, cognitive, and related psychological skill deficiencies among delinquent gang youths have multiple origins, instigators, and maintainers. Such deficiencies, as well as proficiency in alternative, antisocial behaviors, grow first from the powerful and often almost unremitting presence of antisocial models in the three arenas of life in which the youngster spends almost all of his time—family, peers, and mass media. In each of these domains, that is, at home, in school or on the street, and in front of the television set, the youngster is repeatedly exposed to vivid, frequent, expert, and rewarded displays of aggression, egocentricity, impulsiveness, and other behaviors in the full spectrum of antisocial living (Bandura, 1973; Comstock, 1983).

As the youngster himself begins to engage in such antisocial behaviors, he is often much more likely to be frequently, immediately, regularly, and richly rewarded for his (antisocial) efforts than punished for them. Regretfully, aggression pays. Thus, punitive and at times abusive parents, encouragement and examples from peers, and a flood of expert portrayals in the mass media help initiate a process or lifestyle that finds considerable real-world reward—in tangible, social, and self-esteem-enhancing expressions.

The persistence of such behaviors is, at minimum, a joint function of the potency of its roots, the pervasiveness of its reward, and the heretofore relative impotency of intervention efforts. Skillstreaming appears to have been a fine beginning in creating an effective, prosocial-enhancing intervention, but only a beginning. Delinquent youngsters do reliably learn a full curriculum of prosocial behaviors by means of this method, but skill acquisition is not enough. For skill transfer to occur at equally high levels, more must be added to the intervention effort. The roots and maintainers of aggression and related behaviors are diverse and multichannel. So too must remediation be. The youngster must learn not only what to do (a behavioral matter) but also *why to do it* (a cognitive and motivational matter) and *how to control* alternative impulsive and antisocial behaviors (an affective matter). Thus we built upon Skillstreaming, and constituted an intervention we termed Aggression Replacement Training (ART), an intervention that seeks to impact upon youngsters simultaneously along three different but complimentary channels: *cognitive* (via Moral Education), affective (via Anger Control), and *behavioral* (via Skillstreaming). Therefore, we held, to aid in maximizing transfer and maintenance of gain, two additional interventions need to be implemented when dealing with aggressive, delinquent adolescents: Anger Control Training and Moral Education.

Anger Control Training

Individuals may fail to utilize appropriate interpersonal skills because their knowledge of them is weak or lacking, and hence should be offered the kind of performance-enhancement training that Skillstreaming provides. But poor skill performance may also be in part a result of inhibitors to skilled performance in individuals who do possess the skill, at least to some degree. In the case of chronically aggressive gang youths, the target trainees for the present training and evaluation program, prosocially skilled behavior may be rare not only, or because, they are weak in prosocial alternatives to aggression, but also because they have great difficulty in inhibiting or controlling the aggression itself. In addition to performance-enhancement training (Skillstreaming) therefore, such youngsters might simultaneously benefit from training designed to reduce performance inhibitors. Such an anger control training intervention, consisting largely of training in relaxation, self-disputation of instigating self-statements and interpretations, use of calming techniques, and other self-control procedures, has been developed by Feindler and Fremouw, 1983; Moon and Eisler, 1983; and Novaco, 1975.

Moral Education

Kohlberg's (1976) especially well-evaluated approach to enhancing prosocial values is essentially a non-indoctrinative procedure for developing higher levels of moral reasoning. Youngsters are not told in this method what to believe, but instead are exposed to a series of experiences designed to enhance the likelihood that their moral reasoning will progress toward higher, more constructive (just, fair, less egocentric) levels. These experiences, in synopsis, involve first of all the constituting of groups of adolescents currently functioning at two or three different stages or levels of moral reasoning. A series of group discussions then ensues. In these meetings, the adult leader serves as discussion facilitator, not value arbiter of good or bad, right or wrong. The leader's responsibility is to pose moral dilemmas and have them fully examined. These are descriptions of real-life problem situations whose diverse solutions reflect conflicting moral values. Kohlberg and others have repeatedly shown that such moral reasoning discussions, when engaged in by persons at differing levels of moral reasoning, will arouse in many of the discussants substantial levels of cognitive conflict (about their present values), which functions to move them upward, as it were, to new and higher levels of moral reasoning. While this moral reasoning enhancement effect has been a frequent finding by Kohlberg and others, a causal relationship between such prosocial valuing and overt prosocial behavior has been a much less frequent research result. Prosocial values by themselves are often not a sufficient foundation for the emergence of prosocial behavior. It is in part for this reason that Aggression Replacement Training, the intervention central to the present project, also provides the concrete techniques of overt prosocial behavior training and antisocial behavior inhibition.

We have described the rationale underlying our decision to constitute ART with three complementary interventions. In the material that follows we wish to detail the specific procedures that operationalize Skillstreaming, Anger Control Training, and Moral Education. We will follow this operational discussion with a presentation of the actual curricular materials employed when implementing ART.

Skillstreaming Procedures

In Skillstreaming, small groups of chronically aggressive adolescents with shared psychological skill deficiencies are:

1. Shown several examples of expert use of the behaviors constituting the skills in which they are weak or lacking (e.g., *modeling*);
2. Given several guided opportunities to practice and rehearse these competent interpersonal behaviors (e.g., *role-playing*);
3. Provided with praise, reinstruction, and related feedback on how well their role-playing of the skill matched the expert model's portrayal of it (e.g., *performance feedback*); and
4. Encouraged to engage in a series of activities designed to increase the chances that skills learned in the training setting will endure and be available for use

when needed in the school, home, community, institution, or other real-world setting (*transfer training*).

Modeling

Skillstreaming requires that trainees first be exposed to expert examples of the behaviors we want them to learn. The five or six trainees constituting the Skillstreaming group are selected according to their shared skill deficiencies. Each skill to be taught is broken down into four to six different behavioral steps, each set of steps constituting the operational definition of the given skill. Using either live acting by the group's trainers or audiovisual modeling displays, actors portray the steps of the skill being used expertly in a variety of settings relevant to the trainee's daily life. Trainees are told to watch and listen closely to the way the actors in each vignette follow the skill's behavioral steps.

Role-Playing

A brief spontaneous discussion almost invariably follows the presentation of a modeling display. Trainees comment on the steps, the actors, and very often, on how the situation or skill problem portrayed occurs in their own lives. Since our primary goal in role-playing is to encourage realistic behavioral rehearsal, a trainee's statements about his or her difficulties using the skill being taught can often develop into material for his or her role play of it. To enhance the realism of the portrayal, the main actor is asked to choose a second trainee (coactor) to play the role of the significant other person in his or her life who is relevant to the skill problem. It is of crucial importance in the role play that the main actor seek to enact the steps he or she has just seen and heard modeled.

The main actor is asked to briefly describe the real skill problem situation and the real persons involved in it with whom he or she could try these behavioral steps in real life. The coactor is called by the name of the main actor's significant other during the role play. The trainer then instructs the role player to begin. It is the trainer's main responsibility to be sure that the main actor keeps role-playing and attempts to follow the behavioral steps while doing so.

The role-playing is continued until all trainees in the group have had an opportunity to participate, even if all the same steps must be carried over to a second or third session. It should be noted that while the behavioral steps of each role play in the series remain the same, the actual content can and should change from role play to role play. The skill deficiency problem as it actually occurs, or could occur, in each trainee's real-life environment should be the content of a given role play. When the role play is completed, each trainee should be better armed to act appropriately in the given reality situation.

Performance Feedback

Upon completion of each role play, feedback is briefly given. The goals of this activity are to let the main actor know how well he or she followed the skill's steps or in what ways he or she departed from them, to explore the psychological impact of the enactment on the coactor, and to provide the main actor with encouragement to try out the role play behaviors in real life. In these critiques, the behavioral focus of Skillstreaming is maintained. Comments must not take the form of general evaluative comments or broad generalities, but must focus on the presence or absence of specific, concrete behaviors.

Transfer of Training

Several aspects of the Skillstreaming sessions just described have as their primary purpose augmentation of the likelihood that learning in the training setting will transfer to the trainee's real-life environment.

1. Provision of general principles. Transfer of training has been demonstrated to be facilitated by providing trainees with general mediating principles governing successful or competent performance in training and in real-world settings. The provision of general principles to Skillstreaming trainees is operationalized in our training by the presentation in verbal, pictorial, and written form of appropriate information governing skill instigation, selection, and implementation principles.

2. Overlearning. Overlearning is a procedure whereby learning is extended over more trials than are necessary to produce initial successful changes in the trainee's behavior. The overlearning, or repetition of *successful* skill enactment, in the typical Skillstreaming sessions is substantial, with the given skill taught and its behavioral steps (1) modeled several times, (2) role-played one or more times correctly by the trainee, (3) observed live by the trainees as every other group member role-plays it, (4) read by the trainee from a chalkboard and on the Skill Card, (5) written by the trainee in his or her Trainee's Notebook, (6) practiced in vivo one or more times by the trainee in response to skill-relevant events in, or introduced into, his or her real life environment.

3. Identical elements. In perhaps the earliest experimental concern with transfer enhancement, it was found that when there was a facilitative effect of one habit on another, it was both to the extent that and because they shared identical elements. The greater the similarity of physical and interpersonal stimuli in the Skillstreaming setting and the home, school, or other setting in which the skill is to be applied, the greater the likelihood of transfer. The "real-lifeness" of Skillstreaming is operationalized in several ways. These operational expressions of identical elements include (1) the representative, relevant, and realistic content and portrayal of the models, protagonists, and situations in the live modeling or modeling tapes, all designed to be highly similar to what trainees are likely to face in their daily lives; (2) the physical props used in, and the arrangement of, the role-playing setting to be similar to real-life settings; (3) the choice, coaching, and enactment of the coactors to be as similar as possible to the real-life figures they represent; (4) the manner in which the role-plays themselves are conducted to be as responsive as possible to the real-life interpersonal stimuli to which the trainee will actually have to respond with the given skill; (5) the in vivo homework assignments; and (6) the training of natural peer groups whenever possible.

4. Stimulus variability. Several studies have demonstrated that positive transfer is greater when a variety of relevant training stimuli are employed. Stimulus variability is implemented in our Skillstreaming studies by use of (1) rotating group leaders across groups, (2) rotating trainees across groups, (3) having trainees re-role-play a given skill across relevant settings, and/or (5) using multiple homework assignments for each skill.

5. Real-life reinforcement. Agras (1967), Gruber (1971), Tharp and Wetzel (1969), and dozens of other investigators have shown that stable and enduring performance in application settings of newly learned skills is very much at the mercy of real-life reinforcement contingencies. We have found it useful to implement supplemental programs outside the Skillstreaming setting to help ensure that trainees obtain the reinforcements they need and thereby maintain their new behaviors. These programs include provision for both external social reward (provided by people in the trainee's real-life environment) and self-reward (provided by the trainee).

Anger Control Training Procedures

As noted earlier, in contrast to Skillstreaming's goal of facilitating prosocial behavior, Anger Control Training teaches youngsters how to control their
level of anger arousal. Anger Control Training sessions utilize modeling,
youth role-playing, and group performance feedback procedures similar to
those employed in Skillstreaming. As the homework effort does in Skillstreaming, Hassle Logs are used in Anger Control Training to help tie the
training to real-world events—in this instance, actual provocations the youth
has experienced. See Figure 4.1 for an example of a Hassle Log.

In a series of sessions, usually once weekly, participating youths learn a
series of links in a chain of anger-control responsiveness. The first link,
Triggers, is an effort to help participants identify the external events and internal
self-statements that elicit anger. What provokes the youths? Having begun
to master this initial concern, the youths then turn their attention to identifying the particular physiological/kinesthetic cues that let them know that it is
anger, and not fear, anxiety, or any other affect, that they are experiencing. Cues
of anger—tensed biceps, flushing cheeks, hair on neck standing erect, sinking
stomach sensation—tend to be idiosyncratic.

Having identified the stimulus involved (Triggers) and that it is anger one
is experiencing (Cues), youths are taught a series of effective anger-reducing
techniques. In our Anger Control Training program, these include deep breath-
ing, counting backward, imagining a peaceful scene, contemplating the
long-term consequences of alternative behavioral sequelae to the anger being
experienced, and the use of Reminders. Reminders are, in a sense, the opposite
of internal triggers. The latter are self-statements (explanations, instructions)
that instigate heightened levels of anger. Reminders (also explanations, instructions, and the like) are designed to lower anger arousal. Some Reminders are
generic and can be used widely (e.g., "chill out," "calm down," "cool off").
Some are situation specific (e.g., "Jane didn't trip me on purpose, she always
sits at her desk in that sloppy way").

If the links described thus far are used properly, the trainee may reward
himself or herself, a procedure taught as the next link. Finally, since Aggression Replacement Training typically involves youths attending both Skillstreaming and Anger Control classes every week, by the sixth or seventh week
of the program, the youth is armed with a sufficient number of Skillstreaming
skills that he or she can complete the role-playing of an anger-lowering response to a provocation by showing the group the correct behaviors to
use instead of aggressing, namely a Skillstreaming skill. By means of these

Hassle Log

Name _____   Date _____

Morning _____ Afternoon _____ Evening _____

Where were you?

Classroom	_____	Friend's House	_____	Youth Center	_____
Store	_____	Movie	_____	Car	_____
Home	_____	Park	_____	On a Job	_____
Street	_____	Outside	_____	Other	_____

What happened?

Somebody insulted me.   _____

Somebody took something of mine.   _____

Somebody told me to do something.   _____

Somebody was doing something

  I didn't like.   _____

I did something wrong.   _____

Somebody started fighting with me.   _____

Other:

Who was that somebody:

A friend	____	Parent	____	Teacher/Principal	____	Coach	____
A stranger	____	Brother/Sister	____	Girlfriend/Boyfriend	____	Other	____

What did you do?

Hit back	_____	Told peer	_____
Ran away	_____	Ignored it	_____
Yelled	_____	Used Anger Control	_____
Cried	_____		_____
Broke something	_____		_____
Cursed	_____	Used Skillstreaming	
Told someone	_____	skill	_____
Walked away calmly	_____		_____
Talked it out	_____		_____

How did you handle yourself?

1	2	3	4	5
Poorly	Not so Well	Okay	Good	Great

How angry were you?

Burning _____   Moderately   Mildly angry

Really angry _____ angry _____   but still okay _____ Not angry at all _____

Figure 4.1. Hassle Log

components, chronically angry and aggressive youths are taught to respond to provocation (others' and their own) less impulsively, more reflectively, and with less likelihood of acting-out behavior. In short, Anger Control Training teaches youngsters what *not* to do in anger-instigating situations.[1]

Moral Education Procedures

Armed with both the ability to respond to the real world prosocially and the skills necessary to stifle or at least diminish anger, will the youngster who chronically acts out choose the prosocial alternative? To enhance the likelihood that he or she will, one must enter into the realm of moral values.

When faced with the choice of behaving aggressively (usually a richly and reliably rewarded response) or prosocially (often a behavior ignored by others), the latter will be the more frequent choice the greater the youth's sense of fairness, justice, and concern for the rights of others. As noted earlier, in a long and pioneering series of investigations, Kohlberg (1969, 1973) demonstrated that exposing youngsters to a series of moral dilemmas, in a discussion group context that includes youngsters reasoning at differing levels of moral thinking, arouses cognitive conflict whose resolution frequently advances a youngster's moral reasoning to that of the higher-level peers in the group. The dilemmas employed ideally are interesting; relevant to the world of adolescents; and involved with issues of fairness, justice, or the needs or rights of others. Examples of such dilemmas (Gibbs, 1986) are as follows:

Sam's Dilemma

Sam and his best friend, Dave, are shopping in a record store. Dave picks up a record he really likes and slips it into his backpack. Dave then walks out of the store. Moments later, the security officer and the store owner come up to Sam. The store owner says to the officer, "That's one of the boys who were stealing records." The security officer checks Sam's backpack but doesn't find the record. "Okay, you're off the hook, but what's the name of the guy who was with you?" the officer asks Sam. "I'm almost broke because of shoplifting," the owner says. "I can't let him get away with it."

What should Sam say or do? Why? What would be the consequences?

Regina's Dilemma

"Your father called to say he had to work late," Regina's mother told her one night as they sat eating dinner. But Regina knew better. She had passed her father's car on the way home from school. It was parked outside the Midtown Bar and Grill. Regina's mother and father had argued many times about her father's stopping off at the bar on his way home from work. After their last argument, her father had promised he would never do it again. "Do you think I should believe your father?" Regina's mother asks her.

What should Regina say or do? What would be the consequences?

The arousal of cognitive conflict and perspective-taking necessary for the enhancement of moral reasoning is most likely to occur when a range of reasoning levels is present in the dilemma discussion group. For that reason, Aggression Replacement Training Moral Education groups typically consist of 12 members, in contrast to 6 each in Anger Control Training and Skill-streaming. Trainers distribute the dilemma, read it aloud as the youths follow along, elicit a dilemma solution and its underlying reasons from each youth, rate each such response for the moral reasoning stage it reflects, and then conduct a 20- to 30-minute series of debates regarding alternative dilemma solutions among youths at adjacent moral reasoning stages until all have participated.

While moral reasoning stage advancements in youths participating in moral education is a frequent finding, efforts to utilize it by itself as a means of enhancing actual overt moral behavior have yielded mixed success (Arbuthnot & Gordon, 1983; Zimmerman, 1983). Perhaps this is because such youngsters did not have in their behavior repertoires the actual skill behaviors either for acting prosocially or for successfully inhibiting the antisocial. We thus reason that Kohlbergian Moral Education has great potential for providing constructive direction toward the prosocial and away from the antisocial in youngsters armed with the tools of both Skillstreaming and Anger Control Training.[2]

The Aggression Replacement Training Curriculum

Table 4.1 is a listing, respectively, of the Skillstreaming skills, Moral Reasoning dilemmas, and Anger Control Training steps employed by us in our initial ART evaluation research, presented in detail in the chapter that follows. Utilizing this curriculum, our first two studies operationalized ART via a 10-week program; and the specific skills, dilemmas, and steps employed were selected following extensive consultations with a broad sample of delinquency facility staff. Our third evaluation, a longer ART program, expanded upon these contents, and the current program—our fourth efficacy evaluation—is yet a further expansion in length and contents. In this present program, reflecting not only the greater program intensity just noted but also enhanced program prescriptiveness, we have varied skill, dilemma, and step contents from participating gang to participating gang in order to be fully responsive to *their* skills training preferences as the youths themselves defined them. The specific nature of these curriculum choices will be described in Chapter 7. Here, however, we wish to provide (Table 4.1) what we consider our "core" curriculum—used in its entirety in our initial research and in large part filtered into the present program.

TABLE 4.1 Aggression Replacement Training Curriculum

Skillstreaming	*Moral Reasoning*	*Anger Control*
I. Expressing a Complaint 1. Define what the problem is, and who's responsible for it. 2. Decide how the problem might be solved. 3. Tell that person what the problem is and how it might be solved. 4. Ask for a response. 5. Show that you understand his or her feelings. 6. Come to agreement on the steps to be taken by each of you.	1. The Used Car 2. Dope Pusher 3. Riots in Public Places	*Introduction* 1. Rationale: Presentation and discussion 2. Rules: Presentation and discussion 3. Training procedures: Presentation and discussion 4. Contracting for ACT participation 5. Initial history taking regarding *antecedent* provocations-*behavioral* response-*consequences* (A-B-C)
II. Responding to the Feelings of Others (Empathy) 1. Observe the other person's words and actions. 2. Decide what the other person might be feeling and how strong the feelings are. 3. Decide whether it would be helpful to let the other person know you understand his or her feelings. 4. Tell the other person, in a warm and sincere manner, how you think he or she is feeling.	1. The Passenger Ship 2. The Case of Charles Manson 3. LSD	*Assessment* 1. Hassle Log: Purposes and mechanics 2. Anger self-assessment: Physiological Cues 3. Anger Reducers: #1. Deep breathing training #2. Refocusing: Backward counting #3. Peaceful imagery
III. Preparing for a Stressful Conversation 1. Imagine yourself in the stressful situation. 2. Think about how you will feel and why you will feel that way. 3. Imagine that other person in the stressful situation. Think about how that person will feel and why. 4. Imagine yourself telling the other person what you want to say. 5. Imagine what he or she will say. 6. Repeat the above steps, using as many approaches as you can think of. 7. Choose the best approach.	1. Shoplifting 2. Booby Trap 3. Plagiarism	*Triggers* 1. Identification of provoking stimuli (a) Direct Triggers (from others) (b) Indirect Triggers (from self) 2. Role play: Triggers + Cues + Anger Reducer 3. Review of Hassle Logs

TABLE 4.1 Continued

IV. Responding to Anger 1. Listen openly to what the other person has to say. 2. Show that you understand what the other person is feeling. 3. Ask the other person to explain anything you don't understand. 4. Show that you understand *why* the other person feels angry. 5. If it is appropriate, express your thoughts and feelings about the situation.	1. Toy Revolver 2. Robin Hood Case 3. Drugs	*Reminders (Anger Reducer #4)* 1. Introduction to self-instruction training 2. Modeling use of Reminders under pressure 3. Role play: Triggers + Cues + Reminders + Anger Reducer 4. Homework assignments and review of Hassle Log
V. Keeping Out of Fights 1. Stop and think about why you want to fight. 2. Decide what you want to happen in the long run. 3. Think about other ways to handle the situation besides fighting. 4. Decide on the best way to handle the situation, and do it.	1. Private Country 2. *New York vs. Gerald Young* 3. Saving a Life	*Self-Evaluation* 1. Review of Reminder homework assignments 2. Self-evaluation of post-conflict Reminders (a) Self-reinforcement techniques (b) Self-coaching techniques 3. Review of Hassle Log post-conflict Reminders 4. Role play: Triggers + Cues + Reminders + Anger Reducer + Self-evaluation
VI. Helping Others 1. Decide if the other person might need and want your help. 2. Think of ways you could be helpful. 3. Ask the other person if he/she needs and wants your help. 4. Help the other person.	1. The Kidney Transplant 2. Bomb Shelter 3. Misrepresentation	*Thinking Ahead (Anger Reducer #5)* 1. Estimating future negative consequences for current acting out 2. Short-term versus long-term consequences 3. Worst to least consequences 4. Role play: "If . . . then . . . " thinking ahead 5. Role play: Triggers + Cues + Reminders + Anger Reducers + Self = evaluation + Skillstreaming skill
VII. Dealing With an Accusation 1. Think about what the other person has accused you of. 2. Think about why the person might have accused you. 3. Think about ways to answer the person's accusations. 4. Choose the best way, and do it.	1. Lt. Berg 2. Perjury 3. Doctor's Responsibility	*The Angry Behavior Cycle* 1. Review of Hassle Log 2. Identification of own anger-provoking behavior 3. Modification of own anger-provoking behavior 4. Role play: Triggers + Cues + Reminders + Anger Reducers + Self-evaluation + Skill-streaming skill
VIII. Dealing With Group Pressure 1. Think about what the other people want you to do and why. 2. Decide what you want to do. 3. Decide how to tell the other people what you want to do. 4. Tell the group what you have decided.	1. Noisy Child 2. The Stolen Car 3. Discrimination	*Full Sequence Rehearsal* 1. Review of Hassle Logs 2. Role play: Triggers + Cues + Reminders + Anger Reducers + Self-evaluation + Skillstreaming skill

TABLE 4.1 Continued

IX. *Expressing Affection* 1. Decide if you have good feelings about the other person. 2. Decide whether the other person would like to know about your feelings. 3. Decide how you might best express your feelings. 4. Choose the right time and place to express your feelings. 5. Express affection in a warm and caring manner.	1. Defense of Other Persons 2. Lying in Order to Help Someone 3. Rockefeller's Suggestion	*Full Sequence Rehearsal* 1. Review of Hassle Logs 2. Role play: Triggers + Cues + Reminders + Anger Reducers + Self-evaluation + Skill-streaming skill
X. *Responding to Failure* 1. Decide if you have failed. 2. Think about both the personal reasons and the circumstances that have caused you to fail. 3. Decide how you might do things differently if you tried again. 4. Decide if you want to try again. 5. If it is appropriate, try again, using your revised approach.	1. The Desert 2. The Treat 3. Drunken Driving	*Full Sequence Rehearsal* 1. Review of Hassle Logs 2. Role play: Triggers + Cues + Reminders + Anger Reducers + Self-evaluation + Skill-streaming skill

Notes

1. An extended presentation of Anger Control Training procedure appears in Feindler and Ecton (1986) and Goldstein and Glick (1987).

2. An extended presentation of the procedures of moral education appears in Goldstein and Glick (1987) and Zimmerman (1983).

5

Aggression Replacement Training
Evaluations of Effectiveness

This chapter will present and examine the series of efficacy evaluations of Aggression Replacement Training (ART) that preceded and helped to shape both the goals and design of the present project. Some of these investigations were conducted by our research group, a number were the efforts of other, widely disbursed investigators elsewhere. We present these investigations here for what they say about the impact of ART, its apparent strengths and weaknesses, and in preparation for subsequent chapters offering the contents of its implementation and the evaluation of its utility in the present gang-oriented project.

Annsville Youth Center

Our first evaluation was conducted at a New York State Division for Youth facility in central New York State. Sixty youths at Annsville were included, most having been incarcerated at this limited-security institution for such crimes as burglary, unarmed robbery, and various drug offenses. Twenty-four youngsters received the 10-week ART program outlined in Table 4.1. As noted earlier, this required them to attend three sessions a week, one each of Skillstreaming, Anger Control Training, and Moral Education. An additional 24 youths were assigned to a no-ART, Brief Instruction Control group. This condition controlled for the possibility than any apparent ART-derived gains in skill performance were not due to ART per se but, in case youngsters already possessed the skills but weren't using them, simply enhanced motivation to display already learned skills. A third group, the No-Treatment Control Group, consisted of 12 youths not participating in ART or Brief Instructions procedures.

The overall evaluation goal of this project was to examine the effectiveness of ART for purposes of:

a. Skill acquisition, that is, do the youngsters *learn* the 10 prosocial Skillstreaming skills in the ART curriculum.

b. Minimal skill transfer, that is, can the youngsters *perform* the skills in response to new situations, similar in format to those on which they were trained.

c. Extended skill transfer, that is, can the youngsters *perform* the skills in response to new situations, dissimilar in format and more like real life than those on which they were trained.

d. Anger control enhancement, that is, do the youngsters actually demonstrate fewer altercations or other acting-out behaviors, as reflected in weekly behavior incidents reports completed on all participating youths by Center staff.

e. Impulse reduction, that is, are the youngsters rated to be less impulsive and more reflective and self-controlled in their interpersonal behavior.

Analyses of study data revealed, first, that youths undergoing ART, compared to both control groups, significantly acquired and transferred (minimal and extended), 4 of the 10 Skillstreaming skills: Expressing a Complaint, Preparing for a Stressful Conversation, Responding to Anger, and Dealing with Group Pressure. Similarly significant ART versus control groups comparisons emerged on both the number and intensity of in-facility acting out (behavior incidents measure), as well as on staff-rated impulsiveness.

Following completion of the project's post-testing, in week 11, new ART groups were constituted for the 35 youths in the three control group units. As before, these sessions were held three times per week for 10 weeks, and duplicated in all major respects (curriculum, group size, materials, and so on) the first phase ART sessions. Our goal in this second phase was an own-control test of the efficacy of ART, with particular attention to discerning possible reductions in acting-out behaviors by comparing, for these 36 youths, their Incidents Reports during weeks 11-20 (while in ART) with their Incident Report from the period (weeks 1-10) when they had served as control group members. Both statistical comparisons—for number and severity—conducted to test for replication effects yielded positive results.

For reasons primarily associated with the frequent indifference or even hostility of such real-world significant figures as family and peers to newly performed prosocial skills, there is often very considerable difficulty in intervention efforts with incarcerated delinquents in successfully effecting the transfer to community settings of gains acquired in the more protective and benign training setting. Family and peers frequently serve as reinforcers of antisocial behaviors, ignoring or even punishing constructive alternative actions. Our hope was that ART might serve as a sufficiently powerful inoculation, such that at least moderate carryover of in-facility ART gains to the community would occur. In order to test for such possible transfer effects, we constructed a global rating measure of community functioning. During the one-year period following initiation of ART at Annsville, 54 youths were released from this facility. Seventeen had received ART, 37 had not. We contacted the Division for Youth Service Team members (analogous to parole officers) around New York State to whom the 54 released youths reported regularly and, without informing the worker whether the youth had or had not received ART, asked the worker to complete the global rating measure on each of the Annsville dischargees. In four of the six areas rated—home and family, peer, legal, and overall, but not school or work—ART youth were significantly superior in rated in-community functioning than were youths who had not received ART.

MacCormick Youth Center

Our second evaluation of the efficacy of ART was conducted at MacCormick Youth Center, a New York State Division for Youth maximum-security facility for male juvenile delinquents between the ages of 13 and 21. In essence, this second evaluation project sought both to replicate the exact procedures and findings of the Annsville project and to extend them to youths incarcerated for substantially more serious felonies. Fifty-one youths were in residence at MacCormick at the time the evaluation was conducted. Crimes committed by these youths included murder, manslaughter, rape, sodomy, attempted murder, assault, and robbery. In all its procedural and experimental particulars, the MacCormick evaluation project replicated the effort at Annsville. It employed the same preparatory activities, materials, ART curriculum, testing, staff training, resident training, supervision, and data analysis procedures.

On 5 of the 10 Skillstreaming skills, significant acquisition and/or transfer results emerged. These findings, as well as for which particular skills they do and do not hold, essentially replicate the Annsville Skillstreaming results. In contrast to the Annsville results, however, the MacCormick data also yielded a significant result on the Sociomoral Reflections Measure. At MacCormick, but not at Annsville, youths participating in Moral Education sessions grew significantly in the moral reasoning stage over the 10-week intervention period.

Regarding overt, in-facility behavior, youths receiving ART, compared to those who did not, increased significantly over their base rate levels in the constructive, prosocial behaviors they utilized (e.g., offering or accepting criticism appropriately, employing self-control when provoked) and decreased significantly in their rated levels of impulsiveness. In contrast to the Annsville findings, however, MacCormick youths receiving ART did not differ from controls in either the number or intensity of acting-out behaviors. These latter findings appear to be largely explained by the substantial differences in potential for such behaviors between the two facilities. Annsville, internally, is not a locked facility. Its 60 youths live in one dormitory, in contrast to the locked, single-room arrangement at MacCormick. The latter's staff is twice the size of Annsville's and it (MacCormick) operates under a considerably tighter system of sanctions and controls than does Annsville. Thus the opportunity for acting-out behaviors—for these several contextual reasons—are lower *across all conditions* at MacCormick as compared to Annsville, and thus a "floor effect" seems to be operating, which makes the possibility of decreases in acting-out as a result of ART participation at MacCormick numerically a good bit more difficult than at Annsville. At Annsville, such behaviors were contextually more possible at base rate, and thus could (and did) decrease over the intervention period. At MacCormick, all youths started low, and likely for these same contextual reasons (e.g., sanctions, controls, rich staffing, and so on), remained low. Their use of prosocial behaviors, in regard to which no floor or ceiling effect influences are relevant, did increase differentially as a function of the ART intervention.

Community-Based Evaluation
of Aggression Replacement Training

The findings of our first two investigations show that ART is a multimodal, habilitation intervention of considerable potency with incarcerated juvenile delinquents. It enhances prosocial skill competency and overt prosocial behavior, it reduces the level of rated impulsiveness, and, in one of the two samples studied, both decreases (where possible) the frequency and intensity of acting-out behaviors and enhances the participants' levels of moral reasoning. Furthermore, some moderately substantial evidence, provided independently, reveal it to lead to valuable changes in community functioning. This latter suggestion—combined with the general movement away from residential-based and toward community-based programming for delinquent youths—led to our third evaluation of the efficacy of ART, seeking to discern its value when provided to youths ($N = 84$) on a post-release, living-in-the-community basis. We were aware of the potent contribution to functioning in the community that parents and others may make in the lives of delinquent youths. This belief led to our attempt to discern the effects of offering ART not only to youths but also, for training in reciprocal skills, to their parents and other family members. Our experimental design is depicted in Table 5.1.

As Table 5.1 depicts, the community-based project is essentially a three-way comparison of (a) providing ART to youths and to their parents or other family members, (b) providing ART to youths only, and (c) a no-ART control group. For the most part, participating youths were assigned to project conditions on a random basis, with departures from randomization becoming necessary on occasion as a function of the five-city, multisite, time-extended nature of the project. Largely as a result of how long the New York State Division for Youth has aftercare responsibility for youths discharged from their facilities, the ART program offered to project participants was designed to last 3 months, meeting twice per week, for a planned total of approximately 25 sessions. Each session, 1.5 to 2 hours long, was spent in (1) brief discussion of current life events/difficulties, (2) Skillstreaming skills training (of a skill relevant to the life events/difficulties discussed) and, on an alternating basis, (3) Anger Control Training or Moral Education. Once weekly, an ART session was held for the parents and other family members of a sample of participant youths. Those parents selected to participate, but who did not appear, were provided ART in modified form via a weekly home visit or phone visit.

Since the different ART groups that constitute the project's two treatment conditions each chose, in collaboration with their respective trainers, which of the 50 skills that comprise the full Skillstreaming curriculum they wished to learn, different groups learned different (if overlapping) sets of skills. We did not, therefore, examine in our statistical analyses participant change on *individual* skills. Instead, analyses focused upon total skill change for the ART participating youths (Conditions I and II) versus both each other and the no-ART control group youth (Condition III). Results indicated that while they did not differ significantly from one another, the two ART conditions

TABLE 5.1 Evaluation Design for ART in the Community

	Trainee	*Evaluation*	*Condition*
	I	II	III
ART for Delinquent Youths	X	X	—
ART for Parents and Family	X	—	—

each increased significantly in their overall interpersonal skill competence, compared to Condition III (no-ART) youth. A similarly significant outcome emerged (both ART groups versus no-ART) for decrease in self-reported anger levels in response to mild (e.g., seeing others abused, minor nuisance, unfair treatment) but not severe (e.g., betrayal of trust, control/coercion, physical abuse) anger-provoking situations.

A particularly important evaluation criterion in delinquency intervention work is recidivism. The very large majority of previously incarcerated youths who recidivate do so within the first 6 months following release (Maltz, 1984). Thus the recidivism criterion employed in the current project, rearrest, was tracked for that time period. For Condition I and II youths, the 6-month tracking period consisted of the first 3 months during which they received ART, and 3 subsequent no-ART months. Condition III youths, of course, received no ART during the entire tracking period. Analyses examining the frequency of rearrest by condition showed a significant effect for ART participation. Both Condition I and II youths were rearrested significantly less than were youths not receiving ART.

Possessing particular implications for the current gang-oriented project, however, are the trends in these recidivism data discernible in Table 5.2.

Comparison of the percent rearrested rate for the two ART conditions in Table 5.2 reveals a substantial decrement in rearrest when the youths' families (i.e., parent and sibling) also participate simultaneously in their own ART groups. These latter groups, teaching needed and reciprocal (to what the delinquent youth was learning) interpersonal skills, as well as anger control techniques, may well have provided for the delinquent youths a more responsive and prosocially reinforcing real-world environment; for example, perhaps providing a context in which negotiating instead of getting into conflict situations was praised, not castigated. More generally, perhaps, providing a context supportive of, encouraging of, reinforcing of prosocial not antisocial ways of being and doing.

Our present gang-oriented project grows from precisely the same spirit. If our community-based effort captured, as seems likely, that part of the delinquent

TABLE 5.2 Frequency of Rearrest by Condition

Condition	Total N	Rearrested N	Rearrested %
Youth ART + Parent/Sibling ART	13	2	15%
Youth ART Only	20	6	30%
No-ART Control	32	14	43%

youths' actual interpersonal world made up of family members, and turned it at least in part to prosocial reinforcing directions, can the same be done for delinquent gang youths—this time seeking to capture and turn their peer group (the gang) in prosocial directions? Can we, the present project is asking at its heart, not only use ART to teach youths to be more prosocial but, when they indeed do behave in such a manner in their real-life peer environment, can they more frequently be met with acceptance, support and even praise for such behaviors by fellow gang members? A tall order, but nonetheless the ultimate goal of the present, gang-oriented ART program.

Other Efficacy Evaluations

Our three studies of the effectiveness of ART yielded a series of promising findings, both proximal to the ART procedures (i.e., skill acquisition, anger control, enhanced moral reasoning) and distal to it but central to its ultimate purpose (i.e., reduced rearrest, enhanced community functioning). What of the independent findings of other investigations?

Coleman, Pfeiffer, and Oakland (1991) evaluated the effectiveness of a 10-week ART program used with behaviorally disordered adolescents in a Texas residential treatment center. Study results indicated improved participant skill *knowledge*, but not actual overt skill behaviors. Coleman et al. (1991) comment: "The current study thus provides additional support for the contention that although cognitive gains can be demonstrated, the link to actual behavior is tenuous, especially with disturbed populations" (p. 14).

As our own discussion above would suggest, however, we believe that the likelihood of overt behavioral expression (performance) of newly acquired skills is less a function of the degree of trainee emotional disturbance and more a matter of both trainee motivation to perform and staff or other significant persons' perceived receptivity to and likely reward for such overt behaviors.

Coleman et al. continue:

> Of the ten social skills that were taught, three accounted for the improvement in social skills knowledge: keeping out of fights, dealing with group pressure, and expressing a complaint. The fact that Goldstein and Glick (1987) also found these same skills to be improved in two separate studies suggests that these skills may be the most responsive to intervention. One plausible explanation is that these three skills may be construed as contributing to self-preservation, especially within the context of residential or institutional living. (p. 15)

Curulla (1990) evaluated a (1) 14-week ART program, versus (2) ART without the Moral Education component, versus (3) a no-ART control condition. Her trainees were 67 young adult offenders being seen in a community intervention setting in Seattle. She reports:

> Tendency towards recidivism and actual recidivism were compared among the three groups. Tendency towards recidivism, as measured by the Weekly Activity Record, was significantly reduced in the dilemma group [Condition I above]. The nondilemma [Condition II] and control [Condition III] groups showed no significant reduction. The dilemma group also had the lowest frequency of subsequent offense. . . . However, the difference in actual recidivism among the three groups did not reach statistical significance due to the low incidence of recorded changed during the six month followup. (pp. 1-2)

Unlike Coleman et al.'s result, in Curulla's study—as in our own—overt acting-out behaviors were significantly reduced via ART participation. However, unlike our own results, post-ART recidivism was not.

Jones (1990) compared ART to moral education and no-treatment control, using a sample of highly aggressive male students in a Brisbane, Australia, high school. Her results were consistent and positive:

> Compared to the two control conditions, students completing the ART program: showed a significant decrease in aggressive incidents, a significant increase in coping incidents, and acquired more social skills. Students in condition I [also] improved on . . . self-control and impulsivity. . . . ART appears to be an effective intervention for aggressive youth within a high school setting. (p. 1)

A final investigation, also affirming of the efficacy of ART, takes this intervention in a new direction. Gibbs and his coworkers in the Ohio Department of Youth Services had for some years employed and evaluated a Positive Peer

Culture approach in their work with delinquent youths. This technique, described as an "adult-guided but youth-run small group treatment approach," places major responsibility upon the youth group itself for the management of its living environment, as well as change in youth behavior. Feeling that while youths were successfully motivated to conduct much of their own governance and direction, but that they too frequently lacked the skills and anger-control to do so, Gibbs and his group combined the Positive Peer Culture approach with ART to yield a motivation plus skills-oriented intervention they call EQUIP. Leeman, Gibbs, Fuller, and Potter (1991) note: "In EQUIP, moral discussion, anger management, or social skills sessions are designated as equipment meetings, that is, meetings wherein the group gains equipment for helping group members" (pp. 5-6).

These investigators conducted an efficacy evaluation of EQUIP at a medium-security institution for juvenile felony offenders, the Buckeye Youth Center in Ohio. Three conditions were constituted, EQUIP, a motivational control group, and a no-treatment control group. Outcome results were significant and supportive of the EQUIP intervention on both proximal and distal criteria. The investigators comment:

> Institutional conduct improvements were highly significant for the EQUIP relative to the control groups in terms of self-reported misconduct, staff-filed incident reports, and unexcused absences from school. (p. 18)

Interestingly, whereas the recidivism rate of EQUIP subjects was low (15%) at both 6 and 12 months following release, the control group rates worsened from 6 to 12 months (25% to 35% for the motivational control, 30% to 40% for the simple passage-of-time control). This pattern suggests that the treatment result is maintained as a stable effect (p. 19).

The efficacy evaluations we have presented in this chapter combine to suggest that ART is a significant form of intervention. With considerable reliability it appears to promote skill acquisition and performance, improve anger control, decrease the frequency of acting-out behaviors, and increase the frequency of constructive, prosocial behaviors. Beyond institutional walls, its effects persist—less fully perhaps than when the youth is in the controlled institutional environment, but persist nonetheless. In general, its potency appears to us to be sufficiently adequate that its implementation and evaluation with ART groups constituted of members of the same delinquent gang was warranted.

III

The Aggression Replacement Training Prosocial Gang Program

6

Gangs in the Hood

Gangs do not operate in a vacuum. Gangs require an environment and conditions in which to prosper. Gangs form in impoverished neighborhoods, where crime is rampant, access to services is limited, and opportunities for young people to be prosocially involved in their community are limited or nonexistent. In this chapter, we shall explore the neighborhoods in which our program operated and describe the gangs who participated in ART as well as those who served as our control groups. Our effort will be directed at both full description of both gang and hood [neighborhood], as well as how the hoods influence the establishment and growth of the gangs depicted.

The Neighborhoods

Kings County (Brooklyn, New York) would be considered the fourth-largest city in the world if independently incorporated. It has more than 2 million people, 51% people of color, with almost 29% of the population under the age of 21. There are more than 300 distinct ethnic cultures, with literally thousands of neighborhoods (City of New York, 1991). We shall explore but two neighborhoods in this vast metropolis.

Crown Heights

Crown Heights is a culturally rich and ethnically diverse area of Brooklyn. Contained within its 400 blocks is the Brooklyn Botanical Gardens, the Grand Army Plaza, the Brooklyn Museum, Prospect Park, fine residential architecture, and services that include hospitals, schools, community centers, and a well-developed mass transportation system. Crown Heights also enjoys a long history dating back to the 17th century, when it was first settled by Dutch farmers. When slavery was abolished in New York State in 1827, black farmers, craftsmen, and laborers settled in parts of Crown Heights, known then as Weeksville and Carrsville in the Town of Bedford. Across town, industrialists such as the founders of Underwood Typewriter and Gillette Company, as well as merchants such as Abraham of Abraham & Strauss, built their mansions along beautiful tree-lined boulevards. Even then, as now, Crown Heights was a study in contrasts.

Today, Crown Heights is predominantly black (81%), comprised of African-American, Haitian, and Caribbean peoples. There is also a Hispanic population (9%) and a white population (7%). The latter is primarily Hasidim, since Crown Heights is also the world headquarters for the Lubavitch Movement (an orthodox, fundamentalist sect within Judaism). As noted in the Annual Report of the Mayor (Sanchez, 1987):

> Crown Heights is home to a variety of groups struggling to reconstruct this community in their own image. The diversity of these images is both a strength and a source of tension. While fears and tensions are apparent, it is equally clear that the majority of residents care deeply for their neighborhood and are interested in working out group differences. (p. 17)

The citizens of Crown Heights are primarily middle- and low-income wage earners. Through the 1970s and 1980s, a majority of the population in Crown Heights experienced the same changes in their socioeconomic conditions as did the rest of the country. There were increased poverty, decreased purchasing power; more females working, fewer males in the work force; an increase in the single-parent (usually female) household, and a decrease in the traditional family. As in other inner-city areas, housing deteriorated, the population declined, and there was an increase in the use of drugs and other substance abuse materials such as alcohol.

Crown Heights is analogous to *A Tale of Two Cities*. The poorer black community, not well-organized politically, unable to lobby for better housing and secure neighborhoods, lives on one side of Eastern Parkway (a large six-lane thoroughfare that divides the area into two distinct neighborhoods). The white Hasidic (Lubavitcher) Jewish community enjoys a higher standard of living; isolates itself by providing most of its own health care, food, social entertainment, and all of its education; and lives on the other. The racial tension is high between the two groups, jealousy over political connections to the governmental power structure exists, and economic advantage is perceived, so that black and Jewish communities often clash, sometimes violently. Just recently, the killing of a young Jewish student as a reaction to the accidental killing of a young black child caused the community to riot and demonstrate, raising the issue of diversity yet again.

Sheepshead Bay

Sheepshead Bay lies at the southern tip of the Borough of Brooklyn, bordering Jamaica Bay. This neighborhood is part of a unique community that serves three beach areas; it has many tourist attractions, a fishing fleet, the Borough's Community College, and both commercial and residential areas.

The community is comprised of white-collar, middle-income and low-income residents. Approximately 84% of the population is Caucasian, 2.5% is African-American, 6% Latino, and almost 7% Asian. Almost one fifth of the population is under 21 years of age (1990 Census, NYC Department of City Planning). The white population is predominantly Italian, with Jewish and Irish having a sizable representation. There still exists an influx of immigrants, mainly from Eastern Europe and Central America.

Sheepshead Bay also is plagued with socioeconomic blight. There are more single-parent families, suffering from higher costs of living in a stagnant economy. There is a large drug trafficking area on Kings Highway and Neck Road (two major thoroughfares in the community), which supports thriving gang activities. The housing stock is mostly one- and two-family dwellings and six-story apartment buildings. There are no public housing projects in the neighborhood.

The two neighborhoods in which this project was implemented, Crown Heights and Sheepshead Bay, have populations, social conditions, and community dynamics that support youth gangs. Both are middle- to low-income areas that have a significant number of families living at or below the poverty level, high unemployment, little or no industry to support local economies, little resources to provide safe and secure streets, high incidence of drug trafficking and crime. Additionally, social service programs are far less than the demand requires. As such, these localities are ripe for youth ganging activities.

The Gangs

In 1989 there were only 37 active street gangs, with a membership of 1,036, and another 51 gangs under investigation, with an alleged membership of about 1,020, in the entire City of New York (New York State Division for Youths, 1990). By 1993, there were more than 25 gangs in the Crown Heights and Sheepshead Bay areas alone. This proliferation of gangs appears to be due to the underreporting of gangs by community agents, and to the continuing increase of those conditions within the communities that support youth antisocial, gang-type activities. The continuation of poverty, a lack of access to jobs and educational opportunities, a paucity of youth development programs, and a continuing decline of the economic infrastructure all contribute to the development of the gangs in the communities we studied.

The gangs participating in this project had many similarities but also critical differences. The gangs of Crown Heights seem to be more violent, better organized, larger, and far more sophisticated than those in Sheepshead Bay. Those in Sheepshead Bay do not have identifiable leadership and are more territorial in that they overtly identify with the street where they congregate, live, or were formed. Both gang structures reflect their community's demographics, and with the exception of only one gang, are local groups with no national affiliations.

The Gangs of Crown Heights

The Lo Lives: a predominantly black, male gang. The members range in age from 7 to 40. Ninety-eight percent of the members have been or are involved in the criminal justice system and have at least one arrest of record. The Lo Lives have a national affiliation, with its roots in Philadelphia. It is a large organization with several groups in different neighborhoods throughout Brooklyn. It is reported by agency staff that there are approximately 500 members in Crown Heights; 300 members in Brownsville; 300 in Bedford-Stuyvesant; and another 200 members in East New York. That is a total of more than 1,300 members in the Borough of Brooklyn. The Lo Lives are known for "boosting," that is, stealing name-brand clothes, usually Polo or Ralph Lauren. They often recruit their young members from those who express interest in their attire. The Lo Lives started in Crown Heights about 1985, and are not considered a highly violent gang.

The Sammy Dreds: range in age from 7 to 25. The gang has about 50 members who live in Crown Heights. This gang is considered violent and is known for its drive-by shootings, stealing, robbing, wilding activities, and malicious acts toward innocent people. Its members use razors and guns as weapons of choice. As one staff person said: "They will mess you up with no questions asked." They recruit their members from the neighborhood schools and parks. They often deal in intimidation to recruit their members. The Sammy Dreds started in Crown Heights during 1988.

The Brothers' Keepers: range in age between 14 and 21. There are about 20 members in this gang, which is the newest one in Crown Heights, having formed about 1990. Gang members claim that their gang formed because the gang members had many of their family and friends shot and killed. In order to protect themselves, they organized a defensive gang, and only become violent when they are threatened. They recruit their members only from among their friends. The members all wear "hoodies," which are sweatshirts with hoods attached, along with Goretex (shiny clothes) and Timberland boots.

The Baby Wolfpack: an extremely violent gang. There are about 25 members, who range in age between 11 and 30. The gang formed in Crown Heights in about 1982. Each member owns a dog such as a pit bull or a rottweiler. The members acquire the dogs as pups, train them to be vicious, and use the animals for protection and robberies. While the members themselves may not assault others and cause personal injury, they use their animals to inflict bodily harm. The Baby Wolfpack recruits members from those community youths who admire their animals and express an interest in owning a dog.

The Deceptanets: a female gang that formed in Brownsville (a contiguous neighborhood to Crown Heights) at the Graphic Arts High School in 1985. This gang has approximately 50 members, known for their uniforms of jeans and Reebok sneakers, and their hair pulled back. They use needles, Mace, and razors as weapons. The Deceptanets are known to be a very vicious gang whose members rob other girls for their jewelry and ride the subways to victimize commuters. They often stick needles into their prey in order to distract them while they steal the person's wallet. This gang recruits new members through local schools.

The Brownsville Girls: a more recently initiated gang in the Brownsville, Crown Heights communities, having formed in 1991. There are approximately 25 members, who range in age from 16 to 21. They dress neatly and rather conservatively, wearing slacks, blouses, and Timberland boots. Like the Brothers' Keepers, they formed to protect themselves from other female gangs such as the Deceptanets. They do not attend school, although they hang out in front of schools, where they recruit new members. They carry razors for protection, and while not considered generally violent, they will hurt others if they have to protect themselves.

The Gangs of Sheepshead Bay

The Bay Road: a gang in the Sheepshead Bay area that formed in the early 1970s. It currently has about 25 active members, who range in age between 16 and 25. It used to be a much larger and stronger organization; however, police interdiction has decreased the gang's activity and membership. The majority of the members are white and ethnically Italian, and frequently are from the same families (i.e., older brothers and uncles who were once the younger, active members of the gang). Gang activities include burglary and drug dealing, during which the members often harass and intimidate the neighborhood. Unlike other gangs, this gang's violence is sometimes turned onto itself in an attempt to solve petty disputes. Their weapons of choice are guns and knives. The Bay Road gang is aging out because they have no resource for new members (i.e., no younger siblings) and no active recruitment program.

The Kings Highway Boys: started to form in the early 1970s and is similar in its history and development to the Bay Road gang. The Kings Highway Boys range in age from 13 to 25. The group is comprised of family members, older brothers and uncles, all of whom are involved in intimidation and harassment of the community. While the older members are involved in major criminal activities, the younger members are involved with petty theft, auto theft, and petty larceny. There exist subgroups of this gang. Because Kings Highway is a large thoroughfare, those who live on the east side of the highway are known as the Eastside Kings Highway Boys, whose members include African Americans and Latinos. Those who live on the west side of the highway are knows as the Westside Kings Highway Boys and are mainly white Italians. Each subgroup has about 50 members and fosters a junior gang known as the Junior Kings Highway Boys, who are younger than 14 years of age, after which time they "graduate" into the older group. The weapons of choice for these groups are razors, guns (pistols to Uzis), bats, knives, and brass knuckles. This is a violent gang and will cause personal injury to others, unprovoked.

The Neck Road Boys: range in age from 14 to 21. The gang has about 20 members and formed in about 1983. The gang is not an aggressive or violent group, and usually "hangs out" and either uses drugs or deals in drugs. The members may sometimes commit burglaries or other minor offenses. The gang members typically live in single-parent homes, and the gang contains a mix of Italian, Latino, and Jewish members. The gang does not actively recruit members, but individuals may join through a social process of hanging with the group. The group members will protect themselves if they have to, and usually carry knives or brass knuckles for this purpose. This gang is known for its participation in "raves," events where people gather to listen to music and use drugs.

The Avenue U Boys: formed in 1973 from family groups' members. There are about 40 members, who range in age from 13 to 21. Many of the older members (who are no longer active but still affiliate with the group) are perceived as frustrated mobsters who would like to run an organization or club themselves. The gang uses knives and guns, and is involved in intimidation, harassment, and extortion of local store owners. The members include Asians, African Americans, and Italians. Most are out of school and hang out in bars along Avenue U.

The Agencies

Successful youth programs are often dependent upon community-based organizations (CBOs) that are not-for-profit, 501 (c)(3) agencies. These grass-roots service providers range from small "mom and pop" storefronts to large, multiservice institutions. Services provided may be as simple as an after-school tutorial program or as complex as interventions that run the gamut of individual and family health care, social services supports, educational and vocational training programs, and counseling and therapy. The community-based organization network can provide a safety net for clients in need of support and camaraderie, when they are in trouble, or need help in solving problems.

Most CBOs are staffed with dedicated social servants who are devoted to helping others, with little or no compensation. Community-based organizations operate with funds they receive through governmental grants, foundations, private contributions, or community fund-raisers. Within our project, we were fortunate to find two agencies that manifest the essence of community-based organizations, ones that were well in tune with their neighborhoods, had fine reputations with their citizens, and were able to provide the space and talent to implement the ART program.

Brownsville Community Neighborhood Action Center, Inc.: 1757 Union Street, Brooklyn, NY 11213. The Brownsville Community Neighborhood Action Center is a multiservice, community-based organization that has provided youth services to its area since 1967. The agency is supported through governmental grants from the NYS Division for Youth, and the NYS Department of Labor, the NYS Legislature, the State Education Department, and the NYC Youth Board. The Center's purpose is to establish and coordinate youth programs for young people who are at risk of dropping out of school, being involved with the criminal justice system, or participating in antisocial behaviors.

The center has a staff of 50 individuals who operate programs and provide activities that include the following programs.

1.   The Adolescent Vocational Exploration Program is designed to serve youth gang members from ages 14 to 17, and links career awareness with education needs of the youths. Youths are provided hands-on experience in private-sector businesses through field visits, guest speakers, and placements for vocational exploration. Youths receive up to one regent credit for their participation in the summer classroom component, combined with counseling, advocacy, and support services.

2.   Youth Work Skills Program is designed to serve 34 out-of-school, economically disadvantaged youths, ages 16 to 19, who are at or below fifth grade reading levels. Funded by the NYS Department of Labor, the program seeks to improve participants' basic educational skills, job-seeking skills, and employability through basic skills remediation classes, worksite training, support and counseling services.

3. Youth Training and Employment Program is an after-school activity funded by a Special Legislative Grant through the NYS Division for Youth. The program serves youths ages 14 to 21 who are in school by providing career awareness activities, academic remediation, employment training, job training, interview techniques practice, job placement, and public speaking opportunities.

4. Juvenile Justice Prevention Program provides service to 20 high-risk youths from ages 12 to 21. The goal of this alternative to incarceration program is to decrease the number of youths involved in the criminal justice system.

Over the past decade the agency has placed more than 2,700 young people in job training or part-time employment. As with most successful CBOs, the Brownsville Neighborhood Action Center has established linkages with other agencies, such as the Department of Juvenile Justice, the State Board of Education, the New York City Department of Social Services, Crime Victim Services, the New York City Department of Employment, as well as Brooklyn College.

Youth DARES (Dynamic Alternative for Rehabilitation through Educational Services), Inc.: 3154 Emmons Avenue, Brooklyn, NY 11235. Youth DARES was founded 10 years ago as a recreational program for neighborhood youths within the 61st Police Precinct in Brooklyn. The primary goal of the agency is to offer positive alternatives to at-risk youths and their families. Based upon the philosophy that young people need positive role models to emulate so that they are prevented from turning to the streets where they are vulnerable to antisocial behaviors, substance abuse, and criminal activity, Youth DARES provides several core programs for its community.

1. Project BEST (Begin Excelling Starting Today) provides youths with an alternative high school setting where they may earn a General Equivalency Diploma (GED) and participate in educational counseling, and school advocacy. The project provides an alternative setting for those young people who have not succeeded in a traditional school setting.

2. Family Mediation Project fosters open communication in families who experience internal strife. Families meet with trained mediators to discuss their problems in order to identify solutions. Plans of action to implement the mediated solutions are developed and implemented under the supervision of a family mediation project staff person.

3. Court Advocacy Project offers alternatives to incarceration for those young people who are criminally involved with the juvenile justice or adult criminal justice systems. Very often youths are placed on probation and remanded to Youth DARES for educational and counseling services.

4. Counseling Project provides direct individual and group counseling to youths with emotional or other social problems. If necessary, young people with severe psychological problems are referred to one of the mental health clinics with whom Youth DARES has established linkages.

5. Recreation Project of Youth DARES provides basic recreational activities to young people at local school gymnasiums during after-school hours and on weekends.

6. Stars by the Sea is a program in which cultural enrichment activities are provided to youths in the Sea Gate community of Brooklyn. Trips to museums, movies, the theater, recreational parks, and concerts are but a few examples of the types of activities provided.

Youth DARES provides services to approximately 2,000 young people annually.

As can be seen from the descriptions we have provided of the two participating agencies and their programs, each offers a broad and diverse set of creative and useful youth activities: vocational, educational, recreational, and more. Earlier in this book we urged the likely value of what we termed comprehensive gang intervention programming. The rich and relevant programmatic offerings of the Brownsville Community Neighborhood Action Center and Youth DARES provided us with the opportunity to offer and evaluate Aggression Replacement Training to gang youths in the context of just such comprehensive programming.

7

The Program
Management and Evaluation

Program Management

Management of the present multisite, multi-gang delinquency intervention evaluation program required diverse planning, training, supervisory, data collection, data analysis, budget management, and resource coordination efforts. These diverse requirements and opportunities had within them numerous problems to be solved and many valuable administrative and implementation lessons to be derived. In the present section, we seek to share this useful management information.

Program Planning

The present investigation was supported by a research grant from the New York State Division of Criminal Justice Services, a state agency concerned with the creation, evaluation, and dissemination of effective interventions for delinquent youths. As described in the previous chapter, the investigation was conducted at two private, community-based agencies, the Brownsville Neighborhood Youth Action Center and Youth DARES, both located in Brooklyn, New York. One of us (Goldstein) is on the faculty of Syracuse University; the other (Glick) is employed by the New York State Division for Youth. Our point in sharing this listing of support sources, trainee sites, intervention locations, and professional affiliations is to make clear the network of diversely interested parties when one sets out to plan and conduct a research effort such as this. Their interests are substantial and, if not necessarily in conflict, may not always be complementary. Yet all of these interests must be served if the program is to go forward to completion. Thus project managers, starting from the very outset of their project planning, must not only seek to plan good science (design, measurement, and so on), but also conduct skilled negotiation between and among the several interested parties noted above. Our chief strategy for conducting such facilitative planning is *consult and negotiate*. Open, honest, and frequent communication with these several agency and faculty interested parties maximized our opportunity to reflect *their* thinking in program planning and, most importantly, meet *their* needs as they defined them in such plans. Just as in Skillstreaming itself, in which trainee motivation is enhanced when the skill curriculum to be taught is negotiated with the trainee, staff motivation to participate in program procedures, and carry them out with fidelity to plan, is enhanced when major aspects of the program are negotiated with participating staff. Such a planning strategy need not, in practice, negate such research requirements as standardization of intervention procedures, nor disturb randomness of assignment to condition. What it does accomplish, however, is to provide all interested parties with a genuine sense of participation in program planning and shared ownership of program outcomes.

A crucial planning consideration, relevant to both the participatory process just described and the ultimate design of the research to be conducted, is the notion of rigor-relevance balance. Good intervention evaluation research, in both our view and that of the agency and staff collaboration with whom we worked, is both experimentally rigorous and highly relevant to the real lives of its recipients. O. R. Lindsley (1964) spoke of three orientations to experimentation on intervention effectiveness. The "Rigorless Magician" orientation is reflected in the "shoot from the hip," "impressions count for everything" stance held by the individual who eschews objective measurement of effect and relies totally on his or her "clinical judgment." At the opposite extreme is the "Rigor Mortician," so fixated on objective measurement that he or she sacrifices the richness, the uniqueness, and the individuality of the very phenomena being studied in the effort to obtain standardized measurement information. At an intermediate position, and to be recommended, is the "Rigorous Clinician." Here, the balance of rigor of experimental design and measurement and relevance to the real world of those being studied, is striven for. Perhaps aided by the fact that our participatory planning team consisted of both principal investigator researchers and agency staff clinicians, our program evaluation goal clearly became that of the rigorous clinician.

Training, Monitoring, and Supervision

Program integrity, defined as the degree to which program implementation is faithful to, consistent with, or corresponds to program plan, is primarily a function of three related management activities: training, monitoring, and supervision. These functions were initiated with the distribution, to staff at the participating agencies, of copies of the training process manual, *Aggression Replacement Training* (Goldstein & Glick, 1987). This manual describes all ART procedures and their implementation in a highly comprehensive, step-wise, concrete manner. Staff were urged to read and reread this manual prior to the next step in the training process: the trainer's workshop. Here, all staff of the participating agencies underwent an intensive, participatory, experiential series of lessons in the actual conduct of ART groups. These workshops also gave the project managers the opportunity, based on overt displays of ART-relevant competence and incompetence, to select from among the workshop participants those staff members who would actually serve as project trainers, and also to determine, for those selected, which of the three components of ART they appeared most able and willing to lead.

Once the project's ART sessions with participating youths actually commenced, an ongoing process of regular monitoring and supervision was initiated. This process took several forms, depending partly on the physical distance of the facility or agency from where the project managers were located, but also on the developing competence level of particular trainers. Most such monitoring and supervision was operationalized via regular visits to the training sites by the project managers to (a) observe ART sessions in progress and (b) meet with the trainers afterwards to offer feedback. This on-site approach was supplemented by requiring trainers to keep weekly session notes, mailed to the managers for feedback purposes, and by weekly, and often lengthy, telephone conversations. Most of the latter were regularly scheduled, but some occurred, initiated by trainers, on an as-needed basis as issues or crises arose.

Perhaps the most valuable feature of this multipronged training, monitoring, and supervision process was the several and continuing opportunities it provided not only to point out and correct intervention delivery "errors," that is, trainer behaviors departing from ART manual procedures, but also the chance to "catch them being good." Trainers, and participating youths themselves (and all of us), are often especially deserving of, but often do not receive, recognition and praise for skilled enactment of training procedures, which can help maintain and improve performance.

Maintenance of Motivation

The present project was 2 years in length. How does one keep staff trainers interested, involved, and true to intervention procedures as planned during such extended periods? The ART program offered to participating youths within this program was 32 sessions long, conducted on a twice weekly basis. How does one keep youths with short attention spans, most of whom have found antisocial behavior to be consistently rewarding, interested and motivated to attend, participate in, and use the lessons of an intervention designed to teach prosocial alternative behaviors? Our first answer to these often daunting questions, meant quite seriously, is "it ain't easy!" It was our clear sense in the management of this research program that satisfactory program initiation was conducted much more easily than was satisfactory program maintenance. At launch time, often all are excited and eager to "travel." Several miles down the road, when implementation feels routine, novelty has long since departed, and problems—both anticipated and unexpected—have arisen, continuing to be eagerly involved in applying or receiving intervention procedures can and does often become problematic. Below, we wish to share, for both trainers and trainees, the management steps we put into effect to deal with such maintenance of motivation.

Essentially two classes of motivators are at the disposal of any project's management for motivation maintenance purposes—extrinsic and intrinsic. Extrinsic motivators are tangibles provided in advance of or following competent performance. For staff trainers, project grant monies were used to pay for participation. Youths were also "paid," but not with money in their case. Actually, we had hoped to offer them money for participation, but the funding agency disallowed this request. Instead, we fed them and we provided special recreational opportunities, as well as occasional other material or activity reinforcers.

Intrinsic motivators, that is, reinforcers inherent in the intervention itself, or intangibles associated with it, began early in the program's implementation. For staff, as noted earlier, program participation was preceded by motivation-enhancing involvement in program planning and decision making, thus providing at least a modicum of sense of program ownership. As the program developed, for many staff the primary intrinsic motivator became their enhanced sense of professional competence as things changed for the better in the lives of some troubled youths. For the youths themselves, intrinsic motivation followed primarily from their developing sense that the skills they were learning were in fact relevant and functional in their everyday lives on the street, at school, at home, and elsewhere. We promoted such skill relevance and function by regular use of a procedure we term *negotiating the curriculum*. For example, rather than commencing each Skillstreaming session with a presentation by staff of a skill modeling display which they, the staff members, had selected, we engaged the youths in a brief discussion of their current life events and concerns, and from *that* discussion the skill to be taught was mutually selected. Thus a youngster recently fired from his job in a fast food outlet, for telling his boss to "shove it," may profitably choose to learn appropriate assertiveness techniques and thus be taught the skill Standing Up for Your Rights. The shy youngster, wanting to reach out to an opposite sex peer but afraid to do so, will become more motivated to remain in the ART group and learn its lessons if he or she is taught Starting a Conversation and then uses it effectively with that peer.

Finally, as noted above in connection with effective supervision, and as both folklore and several hundred studies of the consequences of positive reinforcement make clear, for both staff trainers and delinquent youth trainees, "catch them being good" was our most consistently effective motivation maintainer. For staff, such praise following competent implementation of ART procedures and, for youths, such approval following competent skill use (or role-playing, homework completion, dilemma discussion, and the like) regularly appeared to promote a desire to continue with motivated involvement in program activities.

The project managers (principal investigators) had overall management responsibility for both agency staff and participating youths and, as just indicated, sought to motivate these parties whenever possible by social and material reinforcement of desired behaviors. But agency staff also had management obligations—in their case hands-on, frontline, or direct care obligations, including the motivation of trainee attendance and participation. It is instructive to observe that the two agencies that participated employed contrasting tactics. One, following the lead we sought to operationalize in our own management style, managed mostly by using the carrot of carrot-and-stick—that is, praise, material reinforcers, communication of both positive expectancies for change and staff availability (and eagerness) to assist in such change. The second agency relied much more heavily on the stick for its motivational effort, primarily reiteration of the judge's threat of reincarceration for failure to attend ART sessions. This latter agency had many times more attendance and management problems over the course of its project participation than did the former.

Coordination of Functions and Resources

As noted at the outset, a number of organizations and agencies were interested parties over the life of the research and evaluation program—a university, a state agency funding source, two private agencies providing implementation sites, interested mass media representatives, a number of local (to the project sites) and state-level political figures. Their interests with rare exceptions intersected and were not a source of management difficulty. Yet they were repeatedly sources requiring management activity. Grant proposals, quarterly project reports, meeting and implementation schedules, budgets, evaluation measures, and other reports, forms, memos, and accountings had to be prepared in an accurate and timely manner. Meetings had to be regularly (and sometimes irregularly) prepared for, scheduled, and conducted, with an eye to both team building and the project's ultimate evaluation goals. The several interested parties—their number and widespread locations— also meant many planned and unplanned telephone conversations; for some, the content mattered a great deal, for others the act of calling was its primary (relationship-maintaining) goal.

Adding to the picture shared here of diverse and numerous management requirements was the fact that the mass media developed considerable interest in ART as implemented with juvenile gangs. Newspaper and television reporters, both local and national, became a presence, to first appreciate and then contend with, over the course of that evaluation sequence. They, too, have their own legitimate needs and demands, but on more than a few occasions their presence functioned as an intrusive detriment to appropriate intervention implementation. Tactful but firm management intervention proved necessary here.

Data Collection and Analysis

In operational terms, managing the evaluation of ART was a multistage process whose concretization, while reflecting the primary goal of standardization across conditions, also had to be responsive to the realities of the participating agencies and institutions. For the most part, however, we were pleased that, even given such realities—for example, staff schedules, other youth programs in operation, confidentiality needs, and so forth—data collection proceeded in a generally as-planned manner.

The specific management requirements constituting this aspect of the program included: (1) the development and selection of appropriate evaluation measures; (2) their duplication for and dissemination to study sites; (3) instruction of site staff in measurement administration; (4) preparing a measurement schedule; (5) test administration to participating youths and staff, as scheduled and in a standardized manner; (6) scoring and recording of the measures thus administered; and (7) conducting appropriate data analyses.

While we had our share of missing answers, no-show testees, last-minute scheduling changes, and similar events, the essential structure of our measurement effort remained intact.

Management Principles

We have sought thus far in this chapter to provide a concrete, nuts-and-bolts description of our research program and its management tasks. In the present section we move to a different level of discourse, to suggest a more general, strategic set of valuable management principles we have both derived from and tried to implement during this project.

Give respect to get respect. The New Testament teaching urging one to do unto others as you would have them do unto you is an especially valuable management principle for successful program implementation. Ideally, the project manager will, with consistency and initiative, need to overtly demonstrate respect for each participating staff member's job knowledge and skill performance. The program implementing staff members, in turn, should be urged to display similarly respectful attitudes and behaviors toward participating trainees' opinions, choices, and overt behaviors. When staff members perceive themselves and their work to be respected, on-line performance of project responsibilities may be enhanced, feedback may more freely be given and received, and staff self-esteem may be favorably impacted upon. Similarly beneficial consequences can also emerge as participating trainees experience respect from staff and one another.

Employ and encourage open and honest communication. Underpinning the effort to promote mutual respect is open and honest communication between and among management, staff, and youths. Not only staff but especially participating trainees know when half-truths are being told or information is being withheld. Such departures from open and "straight up" communication can seriously sabotage important aspects of program procedure. Clearly, we urge, on both ethical and pragmatic grounds, that "telling it like it is" is a wise management principle. Even when it is more work for the person to whom one is speaking, or involves disappointing turns of events or refusal of reasonable requests, open and honest communication must be sought.

Define roles and responsibilities clearly. One of the central matters about which early and open communication is especially necessary is who is to do what, when, and how, as well as who reports to whom, about what, and when. Such clear definition of roles and responsibilities is the backbone of successful program management and must be made explicit as early as the initial invitation to study participation. If offered early and explicitly, discussed openly, and concretized fully so that cross-cutting lines of authority and obligation are minimized, subsequent role/responsibility confusion or conflict will be substantially less likely to occur.

Share project planning, process, and product. In a number of ways, a research program will benefit greatly when decision making about its substance and implementation, as well as the fruits it yields, are not owned exclusively by its management, but instead are genuinely shared. We illustrated this important principle earlier and at length in our section on program planning, and need not repeat such illustration here. We only wish to add that, in addition to such up-front matters as sharing of program planning and process, the sense of ownership and participatory sharing should also fully characterize project products. The products of the present program were both the intangible sense of accomplishment as youths changed, became less aggressive and more prosocially skilled, dropped out of gangs and stayed out of jail, got jobs or went back to school. These were big victories, with credit to all participants openly offered. Such a spirit of shared ownership should and did characterize program tangible products too—invitations to professional meetings, workshops, or other agencies to describe the program and its results; joint authorship of similarly descriptive articles, chapters, and monographs; financial remuneration for some of one's project time and effort; and so forth. Clearly, the shared ownership of project planning, process, and product meant a better project in all three regards.

Program Evaluation

Parallel with our ongoing qualitative estimates of the process and outcome of the current ART program, as described earlier, a quantitative appraisal of its effectiveness was conducted. As in our earlier ART evaluations, both proximal and distal criteria were examined. Proximal to the intervention, we queried: Were skills learned? Was anger reduced? More derivative from the ART per se, we also investigated participant-rated performance in a variety of areas of functioning in the community, and whether he or she was re-arrested during the 8-month period, consisting of 4 months of the ART sequence plus 4 months of follow-up.

Assessment

Interpersonal Skills

The Skill Checklist (Goldstein, Sprafkin, Gershaw, & Klein, 1980; Goldstein, Glick, Irwin, Pask-McCartney, & Rubama, 1989) was our project measure of interpersonal skills. It consists of brief descriptions of the 50 interpersonal, aggression-management, feelings-related, stress-management, and cognitive skills that constitute the curriculum for the Skillstreaming component of ART. The measure's response format permits the rater (in the present project, the agency staff serving as ART trainer) to indicate the frequency with which they believe the youth uses each skill well. In a manner similar to its use in our earlier evaluations of the efficacy of ART, we employed it here on a pre-post basis as our measure of perceived skill competence. The positive outcomes on this measure in our earlier evaluations may appropriately be viewed as predictive validity evidence speaking in favor of its continued employment for program evaluation purposes.

Anger Control

The Anger Situations Inventory (Hoshmand, Austin, & Appell, 1981; Hoshmand & Austin, 1987) was employed as the project's measure of anger control. It is a 66-item questionnaire, completed on a pre-post basis by the participating youths. Its contents are designed to assess both the respondent's overall level of self-reported anger arousal, as well as the degree of anger aroused in the respondent as a function of several different types of potentially provocative situations. These subscales are:

1. Seeing Others Abused
2. Intrusion
3. Personal Devaluation

4. Betrayal of Trust
5. Minor Nuisance
6. Control/Coercion
7. Verbal Abuse
8. Physical Abuse
9. Unfair Treatment
10. Goal Blocking
11. Neutral

Community Functioning

The Community Adjustment Rating Scale, developed by us, was the study's measure of post-intervention community functioning (Goldstein & Glick, 1987). It affords the rater, in this instance the staff trainers leading the respective ART group, the opportunity to rate each youth on the dimensions:

1. Home and Family Adjustment
2. School Adjustment
3. Work Adjustment
4. Peer Adjustment
5. Legal System Adjustment

Recidivism

In the present project, rearrest was selected as the project index of recidivism. Essentially *all* of the youths participating in the present project, as ART participants or control group members, had been arrested at least once, and often several times, in the past. Maltz (1984) has demonstrated that the large majority of previously incarcerated youths who do recidivate, do so within the first 6 months after release. We were able to track participating youths in this regard for an 8-month period—4 while in ART or control group, plus 4 months' post-participation. In doing so, we were not unmindful of the weaknesses of using rearrest as the index of recidivism (Farrington, Ohlin, & Wilson, 1986), but it was the primary alternative available to us, given the realities of the agencies within which we worked.

Results

Interpersonal Skills

Repeated measures analysis of variance, crossing project condition (ART versus control) with time of measurement (pre versus post), revealed a significant interaction effect favoring ART participants for each of the seven skills categories: Beginning Social Skills, Advanced Social Skills, Feelings-Relevant Skills, Aggression-Management Skills, Stress-Management Skills, and Planning Skills, as well a Total Skills score.

Anger Control

None of the resultant ANOVA comparisons on the study's Anger Control measure of ART with control scores yielded significant differences. It is noteworthy, however, that on all subscales of this measure those youths receiving ART demonstrated greater gain in anger control than did control group youths. Thus, although the magnitude of between-condition differences is not significant, its uniform direction may be suggestive of a trend toward the predicted impact of ART on participant anger control.

Community Functioning

Of the five community functioning domains rated by group leaders on the Community Adjustment Rating Scale, only Work Adjustment yielded a significant difference ($t = 2.14$, $p < .04$). Peer Adjustment approached significant difference ($t = 1.73$, $p < .07$), as did weighted score total Community Adjustment differences between ART and control group youths ($t = 1.86$, $p < .06$). The direction of these results all favored ART over control group participants. The significant Work Adjustment ratings result accords well (and no doubt largely reflects) the real-world employment pattern for project participants. For example, in the months immediately following their ART sequence, the majority of the participating Lo Lives left their gang and took jobs in one or another retail business. At an analogous point in time, following their own ART participation, a substantial number of the participating Baby Wolfpack members obtained employment in the construction trades.

Recidivism

Arrest data were available for the youths participating in our first two ART sequences and their respective control groups. Five of 38 ART participants (13%) and 14 of the 27 control group members (52%) were rearrested during the 8-month tracking period ($\chi^2 = 6.08$, $p < .01$). It will be recalled from our earlier discussion that our primary rationale for working with intact gangs in this project was the opportunity afforded by such a strategy to attempt to capture a major feature of the youths' environment and turn it in prosocial directions. Stated otherwise, once the youths have learned given prosocial behaviors, will the transfer and maintenance of them be facilitated or discouraged by the persons with whom the youths interact regularly in their real-world environment? Our favorable outcome vis-à-vis rearrest implies the possibility that such a more harmonious and prosocially promotive post-ART peer environment may have been created. Although it is important that future research examine this possibility more directly, it is of considerable interest to note that very similar rearrest outcomes also obtained in Leeman et al.'s evaluation of ART plus Positive Peer Culture (i.e., EQUIP) as well as in our earlier attempt to create a prosocially reinforcing post-ART environment for delinquent youths by employing this intervention with both them and their families. For these youths (ART for self and family), rearrest rate on follow-up was 15%. For control group youths, the comparable figure was 43%. Both outcomes parallel closely that found here (13% and 52%) for the presence or absence of a rather different type of "family"—the youths' fellow gang members.

IV

Future Perspectives

8

Future Perspectives
Enhancing Generalization of Gain

While the findings of the present project are encouraging and suggest that ART can indeed help gang youths move substantially in prosocial directions, a central issue remains. It is the issue central to all intervention efforts of whatever type: namely, generalization of gain. This topic and means for its enhancement are the focus of the present chapter.

Intervention With the Gang as an Entity

Although our own findings suggest it may indeed be fruitful to intervene with the gang as a unit, both finding and folklore in previous gang intervention research have fairly uniformly held otherwise ever since the purported failure of such gang-directed efforts by detached workers programs (Illinois State Police, 1989; Klein, 1971; Klein & Crawford, 1968; Tognacci, 1975). Klein (1971), for example, observes:

> Another weakness might be termed the paradox of [group] programming. To make significant contact with as many of the group members as possible, a worker comes to depend on group programming, especially in large, traditional gang clusters. This programming may take various forms: club meetings, sports activities, dances, remedial education classes, group counseling sessions, and trips out of the city are common. The paradox, of course, is that those procedures designed for maximizing contact and employing group variables may have the deleterious side effect of increasing group cohesiveness and attracting new boys into gang activity. Most theorists agree that an

increase in gang cohesiveness can be expected to lead to increased gang delinquency. (p. 151)

No doubt there are intervention circumstances (its form, contents, leaders, recipients) for which this now broadly accepted admonition holds. But we believe, too, that there are significant exceptions, that our efforts are among them, that more such exceptions likely exist, and that our collective turn away from the implementation and evaluation of programming directed toward the gang as a whole has been both premature and restrictive of the opportunity to maximize the generalization of intervention-derived gains to youths' real-world functioning.

The Failure of Generalization of Gain

What are the intervention conditions promotive of generalization of gain to both new settings (i.e., transfer) and over time (i.e., maintenance)? Early interveners, especially in the realm of psychotherapeutic interventions, were presumptuous enough to assume that this central question need not even be raised.

Intervention as Inoculation

Many such early interventions—reflecting not only a core belief in "personality change" as both the target and the outcome in effective treatment but also their strong tendency to ignore environmental influences upon behavior —viewed successful intervention as a sort of psychological inoculation. The positive changes purported to have taken place within the individual's personality structure were supposed to arm the client to deal effectively with problematic events wherever and whenever they might occur. That is, transfer and maintenance were viewed as automatically occurring processes. With reference to the prevailing psychoanalytic view on this matter, Ford and Urban (1963) note:

> If the patient's behavior toward the therapist is modified, the changes are
> expected to transfer automatically to other situations. The conflicts involved
> in the neurosis all become directed toward the therapist during the "transfer-
> ence neurosis." They are not situation-specific. They are responses looking
> for an object to happen to. Thus if they are changed while they are occurring
> in relation to the therapist, they will be permanently changed, and can no

longer attach themselves to any object in their old form. No special procedures are necessary to facilitate the transfer from the therapist to other situations if the therapist has successfully resolved the transference pattern of
behavior. (p. 173)

Such purportedly automatic maintenance and transfer, variously explained,
also characterize the therapeutic positions of Adler (1924), Horney (1939), Rank
(1945), Rogers (1951), and Sullivan (1953). In each instance, the view put
forth is that when the given therapy process results in positive intrapsychic
changes in the client, the client is assumed to be able to "take these changes
with him or her" and apply them where and when needed in the real-life environment. As Ford and Urban (1963) note, Rogers, like Freud,

assumes that changes in behaviors outside of the therapy interview will follow automatically upon changes in the self-evaluative thoughts and associated emotions during the therapy hour. Changes in the self-evaluative thoughts
and their emotional concomitants result in reduced anxiety; improved dis-
crimination among situational events and responses, more accurate symboli-
zation of them; and greater confidence in one's own decisions. These provide
the conditions from which more appropriate instrumental and interpersonal
responses will naturally grow. (p. 435)

This intervention-as-inoculation perspective was thus quite widespread
among diverse approaches to psychological change through the 1950s. Because
transfer and maintenance were held to occur inexorably as a consequence of
within-treatment gains, no call emerged for the development of purposeful
means for their enhancement.

Train and Hope

Psychotherapy research as a viable enterprise was initiated in the 1950s
and grew in both quantity and scope during the 1960s and 1970s. Much of the
outcome research conducted at the time included systematic follow-up probes,
which sought to ascertain whether gains evident at the termination of formal
intervention had later generalized across settings and/or time. Stokes and
Baer (1977) described this phase as one in which transfer and maintenance
were hoped for and noted, but not pursued. They comment as follows:

Studies that are examples of Train and Hope across time are those in which
there was a change from the intervention procedures, either to a less intensive but procedurally different program, or to no program or no specifically

defined program. Data or anecdotal observations were reported concerning
the maintenance of the original behavior change over the specified time in-
tervening between the termination of the formal program and the
postchecks. (p. 351)

The overwhelming result of these many investigations was that, much
more often than not, transfer and maintenance of intervention gains did not
occur. Treatment and training did not often serve as an inoculation; gains did
not persist automatically; transfer and maintenance did not necessarily follow
from the initial training and the hoped-for generalization of its effects (Goldstein
& Kanfer, 1979; Hayes, Rincover, & Solnick, 1980; Karoly & Steffen, 1980;
Kauffman, Nussen, & McGee, 1977; Kazdin, 1975; Keeley, Shemberg, &
Carbonell, 1976). If such be the case, these several writers chorused, then transfer and maintenance must be actively sought. In fact, the failure of inoculation thinking as revealed by the evidence accumulated during the Train and
Hope phase, indeed led to a third phase of concern with generalization—the
energetic development, evaluation, and use of a number of procedures explicitly
designed to enhance transfer and maintenance of intervention gains.

Generalization Enhancement

We have elsewhere identified three categories of approaches to the maxi-
mization of transfer and maintenance of treatment and training gains (Goldstein,
in press; Goldstein & Kanfer, 1979). Each rests on a growing empirical base
of support. Their implementation may be sequential or, as we have sought to do
in the present project, simultaneous.

Training Components

The first approach to generalization enhancement reflected in this project
was concretized by our shift from offering Skillstreaming alone as the
intervention, to the Skillstreaming-Anger Control-Moral Education combination that constitutes ART. It is our basic contention that generalization of
acquired skills will be promoted substantially if the trainee is concurrently
taught an array of companion, complementary psychological competencies.

This generalization-enhancement strategy, emphasizing the attempt to increase the level of transfer and maintenance of gain by increasing the potency
(breadth, mode, variety, intensity) of the intervention provided the trainee,
became especially attractive to us as we taught social skills to soon-to-be-

decarcerated juvenile delinquents and sought, mostly in vain for a great many of them, to reach out into their real-world environment in order to bring on board a peer, parent, teacher, sibling, or other to serve as our allies in the generalization effort. For a great many of these youths, no such person existed, or was available, or could be enlisted. We had no one in these instances to serve as real-world transfer and maintenance promoter but the youths themselves. Also, as noted, skills training alone, like essentially all psychological interventions with such youths, too often failed to yield generalization effects. Because of these two factors, the strategy of seeking such effects via increased potency of the youth-directed intervention itself became compelling.

Growing evidence suggests that generalization of gain will be more likely when the psychological treatment offered is both broad and multichannel. Band width in this context refers to the breadth or *number* of client qualities targeted by the treatment; multichannel-ness refers to the range of different *modes* of client response targeted, respectively, by the different components of the treatment. Our approach to chronically aggressive adolescents, Aggression Replacement Training, consisting of separate but integrated weekly sessions of prosocial skills training (the behavior-targeted component), anger control training (the affect-targeted component), and moral reasoning training (the values-targeted component), is an example of such a broadband, multichannel treatment. Demonstrations of reductions in recidivism associated with this intervention are initial evidence of its generalization promoting efficacy.

Training Parameters

A second generalization-enhancement strategy concerns the manner in which ART is delivered. Research in other domains of psychology and education have long established that characteristics of the training process itself may markedly influence both transfer and maintenance. Two such characteristics in particular have proven potent in our examinations of them in the context of prosocial skills training with aggressive youths: overlearning and identical elements.

Overlearning, also known as *maximizing response availability,* involves requiring the trainee to engage in repeated *successful* practice of the newly learned (skill) behaviors, in contrast to moving on to new lessons once initial success on the first behavior is shown.

It has been well established empirically that, other things being equal, the response that has been emitted most frequently in the past is more likely to be emitted on subsequent occasions. This finding is derived from studies of the frequency of evocation hypothesis and the spew hypothesis (Underwood & Schultz, 1960), preliminary response pretraining (Atwater, 1953; Cantor, 1955; Gagne & Foster, 1949), and overlearning (Mandler, 1954; Mandler & Heinemann, 1956). In all of these related research domains, real-life or laboratory-induced prior familiarization with given responses increased the likelihood of their occurrence on later trials. To maximize transfer through the use of this principle, the guiding rule should not be practice makes perfect (implying that one simply practices until one gets it right and then moves on), but practice *of* perfect (implying numerous overlearning trials of correct responses after the initial success). (Goldstein, in press)

In the present ART project, overlearning was operationalized by requiring participants to role-play and re-role-play correct enactments of skill steps and anger control procedures several times for each and every Skillstreaming skill and Anger Control Training procedure employed.

Identical elements, also termed *programming common stimuli,* is the oldest and best established means of enhancing generalization by alteration of training parameters. As early as 1901, Thorndike and Woodworth concluded that when there was a facilitative effect of one habit on another, it was to both the extent that and because habits shared identical elements. Ellis (1965) and Osgood (1953) have emphasized the importance for transfer of similarity between characteristics of the training and application tasks. As Osgood (1953) notes, "the greater the similarity between practice and test stimuli, the greater the amount of positive transfer" (p. 213). This conclusion rests on a particularly solid base of experimental support, involving studies of both motor (Crafts, 1935; Duncan, 1953; Gagne, Baker, & Foster, 1950) and verbal (Osgood, 1949, 1953; Underwood, 1951; Young & Underwood, 1954) behaviors.

In the context of the present ART project, we sought to maximize identical elements by—in Skillstreaming—creating modeling and role-play scenarios (with each youth's help) that felt as much as possible to him or her to be "the real thing" and—in Anger Control Training—by rigorously insisting that participating youths record current conflict events on their Hassle Logs, and use these real-world stimuli as the fulcrum of their own anger control practice.

Training Targets

Although we believe that the alteration of both training components and training parameters, as described above, is likely to increase the likelihood that generalization of gain will occur, in an ultimate sense such generalization frequently proves to be very much at the mercy of the reinforcement preferences and practices of the real-world environment in which the youth lives. Parents, peers, and other figures significant for the youth may respond with indifference, or even hostility, to his or her use of prosocial behaviors. Alternatively, they may be, or may be trained to be, supportive, affirming, reciprocating, praiseful, or reinforcing when such desirable behaviors emerge from the youth. This system-oriented, system-training approach to generalization enhancement, sometimes called "programming for reinforcement in the natural environment" (Galassi & Galassi, 1984; Tharp & Wetzel, 1969) was, it will be recalled, first given expression by us in our evaluation of ART when used with delinquent youths *and their parents* (Goldstein et al., 1989). In one experimental condition, as we described earlier, the parents of participating youths were informed about what the youths were learning, taught how to reinforce it, and taught how to respond with reciprocal prosocial skills when appropriate. Results of that evaluation, it will be recalled, suggested that such a real-world training arrangement had a substantial impact upon decreased youth recidivism.

In the present, gang-oriented project, we sought generalization enhancement by means of a second concretization of the same natural environment strategy. Gang youths hang out with other gang youths. They are each others' powerful arbiters, evaluators, critics, reinforcers. Stated straightforwardly, it was our hope that ART participation *as a gang* would increase the likelihood that, in the youths' real-world environment, prosocial behaviors would be increasingly reinforced (not disparaged), and antisocial behaviors would be increasingly disparaged (not reinforced). Our findings, especially those bearing upon post-ART arrest rates, suggest that a substantial beginning in this generalization-enhancing direction actually occurred.

A Future Perspective

In 1974, Short concluded: "The prospects for channeling the energies of gangs into socially constructive programs seems bleak, because of the operation of group processes, and the limited experiences and social abilities of gang members" (p. 3).

This pessimistic view, which may well have been generally appropriate 20 years ago (before the technology for teaching prosocial skills was in place), is perhaps less broadly accurate today. For some gangs and some gang youths, social abilities *can* be taught. Furthermore, at least to some non-negligible degree, teaching such skills to the gang as an entity can enhance the apparent generalization of their usage in real-world environments. Jankowski's (1991) lengthy ethnographic involvement with a series of contemporary youth gangs led him to note a string of prominent entrepreneurial qualities frequently characteristic of such youth-competitiveness, planning ability, risk taking, status seeking, and desire to accumulate money and possessions.

As Jankowski (1991) comments:

> If there is one theme that dominates most studies of gangs, it is that gangs are collectives of individuals who are social parasites, and that they are parasitic not only because they lack the skills to be productive members of society but, more important, because they lack the values, particularly the work ethic, that would guide them to be productive members of society. However, one of the most striking factors I observed was how much of the entrepreneurial spirit . . . was a driving force in the worldview and behavior of gang members. . . . Nearly all of the gang members that I studied possessed, in varying degrees, [these] five attributes. (pp. 101-102)

Keiser (1969), Padilla (1992), Taylor (1990), and Quicker (1983b) have offered similar observations. Given such motivations, and adding the prosocial comportment and peer support it now seems more likely can be generated, perhaps it is time for the community interested in gangs to more fully examine whether Short is no longer correct. We began this book with a brief listing of at least *some* apparently prosocial gangs. A few contemporary gang researchers have similarly begun to note the positive potential underlying much of the behavior of antisocially oriented gangs (Corsica, 1993; Horowitz, 1983; Huff, 1993; Jankowski, 1991; Light & Bonavich, 1988). We urge further thinking and investigation along such lines, in the belief that such positive potential, when combined with training to develop it and support to aid its transfer and maintenance, may prove to be an especially fruitful direction for future gang intervention work.

References

Adler, A. (1924). *The practice and theory of individual psychology.* New York: Harcourt Brace Jovanovich.

Agras, W. S. (1967). Transfer during systematic desensitization therapy. *Behavior Research and Therapy, 5,* 193-199.

Amandes, R. B. (1979). Hire a gang leader: A delinquency prevention program that works. *Juvenile and Family Court Journal, 30,* 37-40.

Arbuthnot, J., & Gordon, D. A. (1983). Personality. In H. C. Quay (Ed.), *Handbook of juvenile delinquency.* New York: John Wiley.

Asbury, H. (1971). *The gangs of New York.* New York: Capricorn. (Original work published 1927)

Atwater, S. K. (1953). Proactive inhibition and associative facilitation as affected by degree of prior learning. *Journal of Experimental Psychology, 46,* 400-404.

Baca, C. (1988, June). *Juvenile gangs in Albuquerque.* Paper presented at the meeting of the Coordinating Council of the Albuquerque Police Department, Albuquerque, NM.

Bandura, A. (1973). *Aggression: A social learning analysis.* Englewood Cliffs, NJ: Prentice Hall.

Berkowitz, L. (n.d.). *When the trigger pulls the finger.* Washington, DC: American Psychological Association.

Berkowitz, L., & LePage, A. (1967). Weapons as aggression-eliciting stimuli. *Journal of Personality and Social Psychology, 7,* 202-207.

Bernstein, S. (1964). *Youth on the streets.* New York: Association Press.

Bogardus, E. S. (1943). Gangs of Mexican-American youth. *Sociology and Social Research, 28,* 55-66.

Bolitho, W. (1930, February). The psychosis of the gang. *Survey,* pp. 501-506.

Brown, R. M. (1980). Crime, law, and society. In T. A. Gurr (Ed.), *Violence in America: The history of crime.* Beverly Hills, CA: Sage.

California Youth Gang Task Force. (1981). *Community access team.* Sacramento: Author.

Camp, G. M., & Camp, C. G. (1985). *Prison gangs: Their extent, nature and impact on prisons.* South Salem, NY: Criminal Justice Institute.

Cantor, J. H. (1955). Amount of pretraining as a factor in stimulus pre-differentiation and performance set. *Journal of Experimental Psychology, 50,* 180-184.

City of New York. (1991). *Demographic profiles: A portrait of New York City's community districts from the 1980 & 1990 census of population and housing.* New York: Department of City Planning.

Cleckley, H. (1964). *The mask of sanity.* St. Louis: Mosby.

Cloward, R. A., & Ohlin, L. E. (1960). *Delinquency and opportunity: A theory of delinquent gangs.* New York: Free Press.

Cohen, A. K. (1955). *Delinquent boys: The culture of the gang.* New York: Free Press.

Coleman, M., Pfeiffer, S., & Oakland, T. (1991). *Aggression replacement training with behavior disordered adolescents.* Unpublished manuscript, University of Texas.

Comstock, G. (1983). Media influences on aggression. In A. P. Goldstein (Ed.), *Prevention and control of aggression.* Elmsford, NY: Pergamon.

Corsica, J. Y. (1993). Employment training interventions. In A. P. Goldstien & C. R. Huff (Eds.), *The gang intervention handbook.* Champaign, IL: Research Press.

Crafts, L. W. (1935). Transfer as related to number of common elements. *Journal of General Psychology, 13,* 147-158.

Crawford, P. L., Malamud, D. I., & Dumpson, J. R. (1950). *Working with teen-age gangs. A report on the Central Harlem street clubs project.* New York: Welfare Council of New York City.

Curulla, V. L. (1990). *Aggression replacement training in the community for adult learning disabled offenders.* Unpublished manuscript, University of Washington.

DeLeon, R. V. (1977). Averting violence in the gang community. *The Police Chief, 44,* 52-53.

Dodge, K. A., & Murphy, R. R. (1984). The assessment of social competence in adolescents. In P. Karoly & J. J. Steffen (Eds.), *Advances in child behavior analysis and therapy* (Vol. 4). New York: Plenum.

Dreikurs, R., Grunwald, B. B., & Pepper, F. C. (1971). *Maintaining sanity in the classroom.* New York: Harper & Row.

Dumpson, J. R. (1949). An approach to antisocial street gangs. *Federal Probation, 13,* 22-29.

Duncan, C. P. (1953). Transfer in motor learning as a function of degree of first-task learning and inner-task similarity. *Journal of Experimental Psychology, 45,* 1-11.

Edgerton, R. (1988). Foreword. In J. D. Vigil, *Barrio gangs: Street life and identity in Southern California.* Austin: University of Texas Press.

Ellis, H. (1965). *The transfer of learning.* New York: Macmillan.

Fahlberg, V. (1979). *Attachment and separation: Putting the pieces together* (DDS Publication No. 429). Lansing: Michigan Department of Social Services.

Farrington, D. P., Ohlin, L. E., & Wilson, J. Q. (1986). *Understanding and controlling crime.* New York: Springer-Verlag.

Feindler, E. L., & Ecton, R. (1986). *Anger control training.* Elmsford, NY: Pergamon.

Feindler, E. L., & Fremouw, W. J. (1983). Stress inoculation training for adolescent anger problems. In D. Meichenbaum & M. E. Jaremko (Eds.), *Stress reduction and prevention.* New York: Plenum.

Filipczak, J., Friedman, R. M., & Reese, S. C. (1979). PREP: Educational programming to prevent juvenile problems. In J. S. Stumphauzer (Ed.), *Progress in behavior therapy with delinquents.* Springfield, IL: Charles C Thomas.

Fisher, J. C. (1976). Homicide in Detroit. *Criminology, 14,* 387-400.

Fleming, D. (1976). *Teaching negotiation skills to pre-adolescents.* Unpublished doctoral dissertation, Syracuse University.

Ford, D. H., & Urban, H. B. (1963). *Systems of psychotherapy.* New York: John Wiley.

Fox, J. R. (1985). Mission impossible? Social work practice with black urban youth gangs. *Social Work, 30,* 25-31.

Friedman, C. J., Mann, F., & Friedman, A. S. (1975). A profile of juvenile street gang members. *Adolescence, 40,* 563-607.

Furfey, P. H. (1926). *The gang age.* New York: Macmillan.

Gagne, R. M., Baker, K. E., & Foster, H. (1950). On the relation between similarity and transfer of training in the learning of discriminative motor tasks. *Psychological Review, 57,* 67-79.

Gagne, R. M., & Foster, H. (1949). Transfer to a motor skill from practice on a pictured representation. *Journal of Experimental Psychology, 39,* 342-354.

Galassi, J. P., & Galassi, M. D. (1984). Promoting transfer and maintenance of counseling outcomes. In S. D. Brown & R. W. Lent (Eds.), *Handbook of counseling psychology.* New York: John Wiley.

Gannon, T. M. (1965). *The changing role of the street worker in the council of social and athletic clubs.* New York: New York City Youth Board Research Department.

Gardner, S. (1983). *Street gangs.* New York: Franklin Watts.

Gibbs, J. C. (1986). *Small group sociomoral treatment programs: Dilemmas for use with conduct-disordered or antisocial adolescents or preadolescents.* Unpublished manuscript: The Ohio State University.

Gold, M. (1978). Scholastic experiences, self-esteem, and delinquent behavior: A theory for alternative schools. *Crime & Delinquency, 17,* 290-309.

Golden, R. (1975). *Teaching resistance-reducing behavior to high school students.* Unpublished doctoral dissertation, Syracuse University.

Goldstein, A. P. (1981). *Psychological skill training.* Elmsford, NY: Pergamon.

Goldstein, A. P. (1983). United States. In A. P. Goldstein & M. H. Segall (Eds.), *Aggression in global perspective.* Elmsford, NY: Pergamon.

Goldstein, A. P. (1990). *Delinquents on delinquency.* Champaign, IL: Research Press.

Goldstein, A. P. (in press). Coordinated multi-targeted skills training: The promotion of generalization-enhancement. In W. O'Donohue & L. Krasner (Eds.), *Handbook of social skills training.* Boston: Allyn & Bacon.

Goldstein, A. P., & Glick, B. (1987). *Aggression replacement training: A comprehensive intervention for aggressive youth.* Champaign, IL: Research Press.

Goldstein, A. P., Glick, B., Irwin, M. J., Pask-McCartney, C., & Rubama, I. (1989). *Reducing delinquency: Intervention in the community.* Elmsford, NY: Pergamon.

Goldstein, A. P., & Kanfer, F. H. (1979). *Maximizing treatment gains: Transfer enhancement in psychotherapy.* New York: Academic Press.

Goldstein, A. P., Monti, P. J., Sardino, T. J., & Green, D. J. (1979). *Police crisis intervention.* Elmsford, NY: Pergamon.

Goldstein, A. P., Sprafkin, R. P., Gershaw, N. J., & Klein, P. (1980). *Skillstreaming the adolescent: A structured learning approach to teaching prosocial skills.* Champaign, IL: Research Press.

Gott, R. (1989, May). *Juvenile gangs.* Paper presented at the Conference on Juvenile Crime, Eastern Kentucky University, Richmond, VA.

Gough, H. G. (1948). A sociological theory of psychopathy. *American Journal of Sociology, 53,* 359-366.

Gray, K. C., & Hutchison, H. C. (1964). The psychopathic personality: A survey of Canadian psychiatrists' opinions. *Canadian Psychiatric Association Journal, 9,* 452-461.

Gruber, R. P. (1971). Behavior therapy: Problems in generalization. *Behavior Therapy, 2,* 361-368.

Gurr, T. A. (1989). *Violence in America: Protest, rebellion, reform.* Newbury Park, CA: Sage.

Guttman, E. S. (1970). Effects of short-term psychiatric treatment for boys in two California youth authority institutions. In D. C. Gibbons (Ed.), *Delinquent behavior.* Englewood Cliffs, NJ: Prentice Hall.

Guzzetta, R. A. (1974). *Acquisition and transfer of empathy by parents of early adolescents through structured learning training.* Unpublished doctoral dissertation, Syracuse University.

Hagedorn, J., & Macon, P. (1988). *People and folks.* Chicago: Lake View.

Haire, T. D. (1979). Street gangs: Some suggested remedies for violence and vandalism. *The Police Chief, 46*, 54-55.

Hardman, D. G. (1967). Historical perspectives on gang research. *Journal of Research in Crime and Delinquency, 4*, 5-27.

Hare, R. D. (1970). *Psychopathy: Theory and research*. New York: John Wiley.

Hayes, S. C., Rincover, A., & Sonick, J. V. (1980). The technical drift of applied behavior analysis. *Journal of Applied Behavior Analysis, 13*, 275-285.

Horney, K. (1939). *New ways in psychoanalysis*. New York: Norton.

Horowitz, R. (1983). *Honor and the American dream*. New Brunswick, NJ: Rutgers University Press.

Hoshmand, L. T., & Austin, G. W. (1987). Validation studies of a multifactorial cognitive-behavioral anger control inventory. *Journal of Personality Assessment, 51*, 417-432.

Hoshmand, L. T., Austin, G. W., & Appell, J. (1981, August). *The diagnosis and assessment of anger control problems*. Paper presented at the American Psychological Association, New York.

Huff, C. R. (1989). Youth gangs and public policy. *Crime & Delinquency, 35*, 524-537.

Huff, C. R. (1993). Gangs in the United States. In A. P. Goldstein, & C. R. Huff (Eds.), *The gang intervention handbook*. Champaign, IL: Research Press.

Illinois State Police. (1989, January). *Criminal Intelligence Bulletin* (No. 42). Springfield: Author.

Jacobs, J. B. (1974). Street gangs behind bars. *Social Problems, 21*, 395-408.

Jankowski, M. S. (1991). *Islands in the street*. Berkeley: University of California Press.

Jennings, R. L. (1975). *The use of structured learning techniques to teach attraction enhancing skills to residentially hospitalized lower socioeconomic emotionally disturbed children and adolescents: A psychotherapy analogue investigation*. Unpublished doctoral dissertation, University of Iowa.

Jones, Y. (1990). *Aggression replacement training in a high school setting*. Unpublished manuscript, Center for Learning & Adjustment Difficulties, Brisbane, Australia.

Karoly, P., & Steffen, J. J. (Eds.). (1980). *Improving the long-term effects of psychotherapy*. New York: Gardner.

Kauffman, J. M., Nussen, J. L., & McGee, C. S. (1977). Follow-up in classroom behavior modification: Survey and discussion. *Journal of School Psychology, 15*, 343-348.

Kazdin, A. E. (1975). *Behavior modification in applied settings*. Homewood, IL: Dorsey.

Keeley, S. M., Shemberg, K. M., & Carbonell, J. (1976). Operant clinical intervention: Behavior management or beyond? Where are the data? *Behavior Therapy, 7*, 292-305.

Keiser, R. L. (1969). *The vice lords: Warriors of the streets*. New York: Holt, Rinehart & Winston.

Klein, M. W. (1968a). Impressions of juvenile gang members. *Adolescence, 3*, 53-78.

Klein, M. W. (1968b). *The Ladino Hills project* (Final report). Washington, DC: Office of Juvenile Delinquency and Youth Development.

Klein, M. W. (1971). *Street gangs and street workers*. Englewood Cliffs, NJ: Prentice Hall.

Klein, M. W., & Crawford, L. Y. (1968). Groups, gangs and cohesiveness. In J. F. Short (Ed.), *Gang delinquency and delinquent subcultures*. New York: Harper & Row.

Klein, M. W., & Maxson, C. L. (1989). Street gang violence. In N. A. Weiner & N. W. Wolfgang (Eds.), *Violent crime, violent criminals*. Newbury Park, CA: Sage.

Kobrin, S. (1959). The Chicago area project: A twenty-five year assessment. *Annals of the American Academy of Political and Social Science, II*, 322-339.

Kohlberg, L. (1969). Stage and sequence: The cognitive-developmental approach to socialization. In D. A. Goslin (Ed.), *Handbook of socialization theory and research*. Chicago: Rand McNally.

Kohlberg, L. (1973). *Collected papers on moral development and moral education*. Cambridge, MA: Harvard University, Center for Moral Education.

Kohlberg, L. (1976). Moral stages and moralization: The cognitive-developmental approach. In T. Lickona (Ed.), *Moral development and behavior: Theory, research, and social issues.* New York: Holt, Rinehart, & Winston.

Krisberg, B. (1974). Gang youth and hustling: The psychology of survival. *Issues in Criminology, 9,* 243-255.

Landesco, J. (1932). Crime and the failure of institutions in Chicago's immigrant areas. *Journal of Criminal Law and Criminology, 23,* 238-248.

Lane, M. P. (1989, July). Inmate gangs. *Corrections Today,* pp. 98-99, 126-128.

Leeman, L. W., Gibbs, J. C., Fuller, D., & Potter, G. (1991). *Evaluation of multi-component treatment program for juvenile delinquents.* Unpublished manuscript, The Ohio State University.

Ley, D. (1976). The street gang in its milieu. In G. Gapport & H. M. Rose (Eds.), *Social economy of cities.* Beverly Hills, CA: Sage.

Leyens, J. P., & Parke, R. D. (1975). Aggressive slides can induce a weapons effect. *European Journal of Social Psychology, 5,* 229-236.

Light, I., & Bonavich, E. (1988). *Immigrant entrepreneurs.* Berkeley: University of California Press.

Litwack, S. E. (1976). *The use of the helper therapy principle to increase therapeutic effectiveness and reduce therapeutic resistance: Structured learning therapy with resistant adolescents.* Unpublished doctoral dissertation, Syracuse University.

Los Angeles Unified School District. (1989). GREAT: *Gang resistance education and training.* Los Angeles: Office of Instruction.

Magdid, K., & McKelvey, C. A. (1987). *High risk: Children without a conscience.* New York: Bantam.

Maltz, D. (1984). *Recidivism.* New York: Academic Press.

Mandler, G. (1954). Transfer of training as a function of degree of response overlearning. *Journal of Experimental Psychology, 47,* 411-417.

Mandler, G., & Heinemann, S. H. (1956). Effect of overlearning of a verbal response on transfer of training. *Journal of Experimental Psychology, 52,* 39-46.

Mattick, H. W., & Caplan, N. S. (1962). *Chicago youth development project: The Chicago boys club.* Ann Arbor, MI: Institute for Social Research.

Maxson, C. L., Gordon, M. A., & Klein, M. W. (1985). Differences between gang and non-gang homicides. *Criminology, 23,* 209-221.

Maxson, C. L., & Klein, M. W. (1983). Gangs, why we couldn't stay away. In J. R. Kleugel (Ed.), *Evaluating juvenile justice.* Beverly Hills, CA: Sage.

McCord, W., & McCord, J. (1964). *The psychopath: An essay on the criminal mind.* Princeton, NJ: Van Nostrand.

Miller, W. B. (1970). Youth gangs in the urban crisis era. In J. F. Short (Ed.), *Delinquency, crime and society.* Chicago: University of Chicago Press.

Miller, W. B. (1974). American youth gangs: Past and present. In A. Blumberg (Ed.), *Current perspectives on criminal behavior.* New York: Knopf.

Miller, W. B. (1975). *Violence by youth gangs and youth groups as a crime problem in major American cities.* Washington, DC: National Institute for Juvenile Justice and Delinquency Prevention.

Miller, W. B. (1982). *Crime by youth gangs and groups in the United States.* Washington, DC: National Institute for Juvenile Justice and Delinquency Prevention.

Miller, W. B., Geertz, H., & Cutter, H.S.G. (1968). Aggression in a boys' street-corner group. In J. F. Short (Ed.), *Gang delinquency and delinquent subcultures.* New York: Harper & Row.

Moon, J. R., & Eisler, R. M. (1983). Anger control: An experimental comparison of three behavioral treatments. *Behavior Therapy, 14,* 493-505.

Moore, J. W., Garcia, R., Garcia, C., Cerda, L., & Valencia, F. (1978). *Homeboys, gangs, drugs, and prison in the barrios of Los Angeles*. Philadelphia: Temple University Press.

Moore, J. W., Vigil, D., & Garcia, R. (1983). Residence and territoriality in Chicano gangs. *Social Problems, 31*, 182-194.

Morales, A. (1981). *Treatment of Hispanic gang members*. Los Angeles: University of California Neuropsychiatric Institute.

Mulvihill, D. J., Tumin, N. M., & Curtis, L. A. (1969). *Crimes of violence*. Washington, DC: National Commission on the Causes and Prevention of Violence.

Needle, J. A., & Stapleton, W. V. (1982). *Police handling youth gangs*. Washington, DC: National Juvenile Justice Assessment Center.

New York City Youth Board. (1960). *Reaching the fighting gang*. New York: Author.

New York State Division for Youth. (1990). *Reaffirming prevention: Report of the Task Force on Juvenile Gangs*. Albany: Author.

Novaco, R. W. (1975). *Anger control: The development and evaluation of an experimental treatment*. Lexington, MA: D. C. Heath.

O'Leary, K. D., O'Leary, S., & Becker, W. C. (1967). Modification of a deviant sibling interaction pattern in the home. *Behavior Research and Therapy, 5*, 113-120.

Osgood, C. E. (1949). The similarity paradox in human learning: A resolution. *Psychological Review, 56*, 132-143.

Osgood, C. E. (1953). *Method and theory in experimental psychology*. New York: Oxford University Press.

Padilla, F. M. (1992). *The gang as an American enterprise*. New Brunswick, NJ: Rutgers University Press.

Patterson, G. R., Cobb, J. A., & Ray, R. S. (1973). A social engineering technology for retraining the families of aggressive boys. In H. E. Adams & I. P. Unikel (Eds.), *Issues and trends in behavior therapy*. Springfield, IL: Charles C Thomas.

Puffer, J. A. (1912). *The boy and his gang*. Boston: Houghton Mifflin.

Quicker, J. C. (1983a). *Homegirls: Characterizing Chicano gangs*. San Pedro, CA: International Universities Press.

Quicker, J. C. (1983b). *Seven decades of gangs*. Sacramento: State of California Commission on Crime Control and Violence Prevention.

Raleigh, R. (1977). *Individual versus group structured learning therapy for assertiveness training with senior and junior high school students*. Unpublished doctoral dissertation, Syracuse University.

Rank, O. (1945). *Will therapy*. New York: Knopf.

Redl, F., & Wineman, D. (1957). *The aggressive child*. New York: Free Press.

Reissman, F. (1965). The helper therapy principle. *Social Work, 10*, 27-32.

Reuterman, N. A. (1975). Formal theories of gangs. In D. Cartwright, B. Thomson, & H. Shwartz (Eds.), *Gang delinquency*. Pacific Grove, CA: Brooks/Cole.

Rogers, C. R. (1951). *Client-centered therapy: Its practice, implications, and theory*. Boston: Houghton Mifflin.

Rogers, C. R. (1957). The necessary and sufficient conditions of therapeutic personality change. *Journal of Consulting Psychology, 21*, 95-103.

Rutter, M. (1980). *Changing youth in a changing society*. Cambridge, MA: Harvard University Press.

Sanchez, T. (1987). *The Crown Heights neighborhood profile*. Brooklyn, NY: Brooklyn in Touch Information Center.

San Diego Association of State Governments. (1982). *Juvenile violence and gang-related crime*. San Diego, CA: Author.

Shaw, C. R., & McKay, H. D. (1942). *Juvenile delinquency and urban areas: A study of rates of delinquency in relation to differential characteristics of local communities in American cities.* Chicago: University of Chicago Press.

Sheldon, W. H. (1949). *Varieties of delinquent youth.* New York: Harper.

Short, J. F. (1974). Youth gangs and society: Micro- and macrosociological processes. *The Sociological Quarterly, 15,* 3-19.

Slavson, S. R. (1964). *A textbook in analytic group psychotherapy.* New York: International Universities Press.

Solomon, E. (1978). *Structural learning therapy with abusive parents.* Unpublished doctoral dissertation, Syracuse University.

Spergel, I. A. (1965). *Street gang work: Theory and practice.* Reading, MA: Addison-Wesley.

Spergel, I. A. (1986). *The violent gang problem in Chicago.* Chicago: University of Chicago, School of Social Service Administration.

Spergel, I. A., & Curry, G. D. (1990). *Survey of youth gang problems and programs in 45 cities and 6 sites.* Washington, DC: Office of Juvenile Justice and Delinquency Prevention.

Spergel, I. A., Ross, R. E., Curry, G. D., & Chance, R. (1989). *Youth gangs: Problem and response.* Washington, DC: Office of Juvenile Justice and Delinquency Prevention.

Stokes, T. F., & Baer, D. M. (1977). An implicit technology of generalization. *Journal of Applied Behavior Analysis, 10,* 349-367.

Stuart, R. B., Jayaratne, S., & Tripoldi, T. (1976). Changing adolescent deviant behavior through reprogramming the behavior of parents and teachers. *Canadian Journal of Behavioral Science, 8,* 132-144.

Sturm, D. (1979). *Therapist aggression tolerance and dependent tolerance under standardized conditions of hostility and dependency.* Unpublished doctoral dissertation, Syracuse University.

Sullivan, H. S. (1953). *Conceptions of modern psychiatry.* New York: Norton.

Sweeney, T. (1981). *Streets of anger, streets of hope: Youth gangs in East Los Angeles.* Glendale, CA: Great Western Publishing.

Tannenbaum, F. (1938). *Crime and the community.* Boston: Ginn.

Taylor, C. S. (1990). Gang imperialism. In C. R. Huff (Ed.), *Gangs in America.* Newbury Park, CA: Sage.

Tharp, R. G., & Wetzel, R. J. (1969). *Behavior modification in the natural environment.* New York: Academic Press.

Thompson, D. W., & Jason, L. A. (1988). Street gangs and preventive interventions. *Criminal Justice and Behavior, 15,* 323-333.

Thorndike, E. L., & Woodworth, R. S. (1901). The influence of improvement in one mental function upon the efficiency of other functions. *Psychological Review, 8,* 247-261.

Thrasher, F. M. (1927). *The gang.* Chicago: University of Chicago Press. (Reprinted 1963).

Tognacci, L. (1975). Pressures toward uniformity in delinquent gangs. In D. S. Cartwright, B. Thomson, & H. Shwartz (Eds.), *Gang delinquency.* Pacific Grove, CA: Brooks/Cole.

Torchia, J. R. (1980, December). Ocean Township Youth Volunteer Corps. *Law and Order,* pp. 12-15.

Tracy, P. E. (1979). *Subcultural delinquency: A comparison of the incidence and seriousness of gang and nongang member offensivity.* Philadelphia: University of Pennsylvania, Center for Studies in Criminology and Criminal Law.

Trief, P. (1976). *The reduction of egocentrism in acting-out adolescents by structured learning therapy.* Unpublished doctoral dissertation, Syracuse University.

Truax, C. B., Wargo, D. G., & Silber, L. D. (1966). Effects of group psychotherapy with high accurate empathy and nonresponsive warmth upon female institutionalized delinquents. *Journal of Abnormal Psychology, 71,* 267-274.

Turner, C. W., Simons, L. S., Berkowitz, L., & Frodi, A. (1977). The stimulating and inhibiting effects of weapons on aggressive behavior. *Aggressive Behavior, 3*, 355-378.

Underwood, B. J. (1951). Associative transfer in verbal learning as a function of response similarity and degree of first-list learning. *Journal of Experimental Psychology, 42*, 44-53.

Underwood, B. J., & Schultz, R. W. (1960). *Meaningfulness and verbal behavior.* New York: Lippincott.

Vigil, J. D. (1983). Chicano gangs: One response to Mexican urban adaptation in the Los Angeles area. *Urban Anthropology, 12*, 45-75.

Vigil, J. D. (1988). *Barrio gangs: Street life and identity in Southern California.* Austin: University of Texas Press.

Walker, H. M. (1979). *The acting-out child: Coping with classroom disruption.* Boston: Allyn & Bacon.

Wattenberg, W. W., & Balistrieri, J. J. (1950). Gangs membership and juvenile misconduct. *American Sociological Review, 15*, 181-186.

Willis-Kistler, P. (1988, November). Fighting gangs with recreation. *P&R*, 45-49.

Willman, M. T., & Snortum, J. R. (1982). A police program for employment of youth gang members. *International Journal of Offender Therapy and Comparative Criminology, 26*, 207-214.

Yablonsky, L. (1967). *The violent gang.* New York: Penguin.

Young, R. K., & Underwood, B. J. (1954). Transfer in verbal materials with dissimilar stimuli and response similarity varied. *Journal of Experimental Psychology, 47*, 153-159.

Zimmerman, D. (1983). Moral education. In Center for Research on Aggression (Ed.), *Prevention and control of aggression.* Elmsford, NY: Pergamon.

Zimring, F. (1977). Determinants of the death rate from robbery. *Journal of Legal Studies, 6*, 317-332.

Author Index

Subject Index

levels/forms of, 13-16
provocations, 21-22

Weaponry, 18

Youth DARES (Dynamic Alternative for Re-
    habilitation through Education Serv-
    ices), 83-84, 85

About the Authors

Arnold P. Goldstein is Professor of Special Education at Syracuse University and Director of their Center for Research on Aggression. He also directs the New York State Taskforce on Juvenile Gangs and is a member of the American Psychological Association Commission on Youth Violence.

Barry Glick is Associate Deputy Director for Local Services, New York State Division for Youth, and former Executive Director of the Annsville Youth Center and Elmcrest Children's Center, both New York residential facilities for delinquent youths.

Wilma Carthan is Executive Director, Brownsville Community Neighborhood Action Center, a multiservice agency in Brooklyn, New York, providing employment, family, and educational services to high-risk minority youths.

Douglas A. Blancero is Executive Director, Youth DARES (Dynamic Alternative for Rehabilitation through Educational Services), a Brooklyn, New York, organization offering advocacy, counseling, and mediation services to youngsters experiencing difficulty in family, legal, school, and peer contexts.